THE
HYPERINFLATION
S U R V I V A L   G U I D E

Strategies for American Businesses

By Gerald Swanson, Ph.D.
Economist — University of Arizona,
College of Business and Public Administration

Sponsored by  FIGGIE INTERNATIONAL

Published by Eric Englund
  5042-A Foothills Rd.
  Lake Oswego, OR 97034

ISBN: 0-9741180-1-X

We would like to acknowledge our gratitude to the many firms and individuals that allowed us to interview them, and kindly extended themselves to give us every assistance.

We would especially like to thank the Bank of Boston and Arthur Andersen in both Argentina and Brazil, without whom this study would not have been possible.

We also want to express our appreciation to all those who helped research, write and edit this book, particularly Rich Bezjak, Scott Chaikin and Adam Snyder.

Table of Contents

Preface

By
Harry E. Figgie, Jr.
Chairman and Chief Executive Officer
Figgie International Inc.

Imagine that a customer has just placed the largest order you have ever received, and he is prepared to pay cash for immediate delivery.

Your response? You thank him and explain that you can't afford to fill the order, in spite of the fact that you have enough inventory.

You explain further that you gave your employees a 10 percent pay hike last week, and they will be demanding another within the month.

The price of your most important raw material went up 12 percent yesterday, and to purchase more you will need a loan, with interest rates currently running at 6 percent *monthly*.

In spite of your increased wage and supply costs, you can't raise your own prices because the government refused your latest price increase request.

If you fill your customer's order, you will actually lose money.

This scenario, in one form or another, is not uncommon in economies with soaring inflation rates, and has become practically routine in countries like Brazil, Argentina and Bolivia.

But I am not asking you to imagine what it would be like to run a business in South America, where the situation is often worse than the one I just described.

I am asking you to imagine what it might one day be like in the United States.

If the U.S. fails to rein in its debt — the largest in world history and more than double the debt of the entire Third World — American businesses might find themselves facing South America's inflationary nightmare.

The United States has destroyed its economic flexibility, and the longer we wait to confront our problems, the more impossible they will be to overcome.

Between 1982 and 1987, the U.S. debt more than doubled, climbing from just over $1 trillion to almost $2.4 trillion. Projections suggest that, if current trends are allowed to continue, that debt could reach $13 trillion by the year 2000. At that point, our annual deficit would be as much as $2 trillion, and *$1.6 trillion* of that would simply be interest on the debt!

American industry is in similar straits. As of mid-1988, corporate debt had reached $1.8 trillion, and U.S. non-financial industry had a debt-to-equity ratio of 0.9 to 1, the highest in history. The pre-tax earnings coverage of interest had fallen from 26 times to only two.

I am basically a businessman, and I don't consider myself an alarmist. However, as part of our corporate planning process, Figgie International has been forced to face the strong possibility that we will be thrust into a high inflationary climate by the middle of the 1990s.

We decided a couple of years ago to prepare for that prospect, and began looking for information on how companies operate during hyperinflation. Unfortunately, we found that very little had been written on that subject in the United States.

As a result, we initiated research of our own, and chose as our target South America — specifically Bolivia, Brazil and Argentina — as the best available example of economies suffering high inflation rates.

We put together a three-person team headed by Dr. Gerald Swanson, a University of Arizona economist and director of the Academy for Economic Education.

The team went to South America four times over a two-year period to study the development of inflation and its impact on businesses, individuals and governments. They interviewed 80 leading bankers and industrialists and a considerable number of ordinary citizens throughout Argentina, Brazil and Bolivia.

The team's findings were quite frightening.

First of all, many of the South Americans are convinced that the United States is following the same path their countries followed, and cannot believe we don't see what lies ahead. They are absolutely amazed, for example, that U.S. banks still offer 30-year, fixed-rate loans. When their pre-hyperinflationary economies are compared to our current economy, it is difficult to argue that they are wrong.

Nor are they alone in thinking the United States is headed toward disaster. During a recent round of meetings we had with European financial leaders, concerns over the fiscal irresponsibility of the U.S. government were raised again and again. And, following Black Monday in October 1987, the head of virtually every major free country spoke out about the need for the U.S. to attack its deficit, though there is little indication the deficit had anything to do with the market crash.

Another sobering discovery the team made in South America was that inflation can accelerate without warning into hyperinflation — or severe, debilitating inflation — in a period as short as a few days.

They also found that the impact of hyperinflation on business management is tremendous, often forcing companies to change the basic focus of their businesses. During periods of runaway inflation, there is no stability: prices skyrocket, supplies dry up, and government intervention is the rule. Survival becomes the sole objective, and production and sales are often neglected in favor of speculation.

One of the most unsettling discoveries the team made was that successful South American individuals and businesses survive by investing in dollars. As a matter of fact, the manager of a South American tennis club reported that 95 percent of the members had paid their most recent dues increases with checks drawn on American banks. Should inflation take off in the United States, we will have no alternative currency to turn to. The first few companies will arbitrage against the Swiss franc, the Dutch guilder or the German mark, but the rest of us probably won't have much choice except to hedge against commodities.

The South Americans almost unanimously agree that the best way to fight hyperinflation is to keep it from starting, because once it begins, it feeds on itself and is extremely difficult to stop. They also say that, once inflation rates do begin to spiral upward, three steps are required: restrict government spending and subsidies, control the money supply, and privatize government businesses to the maximum extent.

Obviously, only the government can do what is necessary to avoid or curb high inflation. All industry or individuals can do — other than pressing for government action — is to cope with the results. This manual is designed to help managers do just that. It offers an extensive list of insights into how American businesses can best survive high inflation, covering the areas of financial management, marketing, manufacturing and industrial relations. The strategies discussed are based on the experiences of South American business leaders who have battled long and successfully with some of the highest inflation rates in recent world history.

Though this manual focuses on inflation's impact on businesses, we are also planning a companion volume that will discuss inflation's development and its effects on individuals and governments. The picture in those areas is no brighter: Pensions, savings, bonds and insurance policies become absolutely worthless. Credit is virtually nonexistent, and people must pay cash for everything — including houses. Wages never keep step with prices, which rise continually. In an Argentine supermarket, it was common to take a loaf of bread from the shelf, only to find that the price had increased by the time it reached the checkout counter.

It is my fervent hope that this manual will turn out to be interesting, but unnecessary. However, to ignore South America's lessons — and warnings — is to hide one's head in the sand. At Figgie International, we plan to prepare ourselves for the very real possibility that the U.S. inflation rate will soon take off, and we offer this manual to other American businesses in the hopes that all of us can survive whatever curves the U.S. economy may throw.

WHAT EXACTLY IS HYPERINFLATION?

The classic definition of hyperinflation, as described in 1956 by economist Phillip Cagan, is a 50 percent average monthly price rise, translating into an annual inflation rate of 12,875 percent compounded. While Bolivia met that criterion in 1985, Argentina's and Brazil's inflation peaked at 20 to 25 percent monthly, or 800 to 1,400 percent annualized. Still, this was sufficient to wreak havoc on all three economies. For the purposes of this report, "hyperinflation" is used to signify rapid, debilitating inflation that leads to a major devaluation of a country's currency, which happened in all three countries.

Introduction

"The problem with hyperinflation is that it happens so fast. We never realized what was happening until it was too late."
— *South American bank director*

"Sometimes I wonder how the United States holds together. Your investments in productive assets are down, growth in non-productive sectors is up, and you purchase more than you produce."
— *South American bank director*

"In South America, taking a cab is cheaper than a bus because you pay for the cab at the end of the ride. By then, the money is worth less."
— *Common saying*

Once the chief scourge of every respectable U.S. economist, inflation has become the forgotten bandit of the eighties. Though occasionally discussed in the back pages of the press, inflation has been supplanted in the public consciousness by issues like America's dwindling global competitiveness, recessionary trends, and foreign trade imbalance.

The primary reason inflationary concerns have abated is that, contrary to traditional economic theory, the huge U.S. budget

1

deficits of the past few years have not translated into spiraling prices.

The continuing failure of our deficits to trigger inflation has confounded many economists, because the postwar years, until this decade, have demonstrated a direct correlation between the two. When deficits rose, increases in prices and interest rates were sure to follow. Since 1980, however, the annual deficit has tripled and the national debt has doubled, yet nominal interest rates have actually fallen.

Many economists believe the U.S. has avoided inflation only because the other developed nations of the world have been willing to finance our excesses. Whatever the reason for this aberration, we can consider ourselves fortunate. However, most economists would argue that the trend is simply not sustainable.

South America: A Frightening Lesson

Observers of the South American economic scene may feel a special horror as the U.S. government continues to add to its mountain of debt. Countries such as Brazil, Argentina and Bolivia have for years demonstrated similar deficit-spending habits, each with the same result — runaway inflation. All three nations have suffered triple- or quadruple-digit inflation in recent years. As a matter of fact, in the case of Bolivia, the inflation rate has climbed as high as 25,000 percent, topping out at a monthly annualized rate of 50,000 percent during the spring of 1985. Not only is this among the highest inflation rates in world history, but it is believed to be the highest ever for a peacetime economy. (Exhibit 1 on the next page gives an illustration of the tremendous impact inflation has had on the cost of living in each country.)

To learn more about functioning in a severely inflationary environment, a three-person research team spent a total of eight weeks in these three countries on four separate trips: May 1986, January 1987, May 1987 and January 1988. Personal, in-depth interviews were conducted with 80 of the leading bankers, economists and businessmen in Argentina, Bolivia and Brazil. Interviewees included top executives of large, publicly and privately held companies, banks and accounting firms, some of them South American-owned and others South American branches of major U.S.-based companies.

There is widespread agreement among these South American economists, bankers and business executives that the principal

2

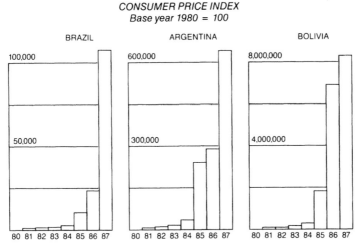

CONSUMER PRICE INDEX
Base year 1980 = 100

BRAZIL · ARGENTINA · BOLIVIA

Exhibit 1: *These charts show the massive increases in prices experienced in all three countries during the 1980s. In Bolivia, for example, an item valued at 100 pesos in 1980 cost the equivalent of over eight million pesos by 1987.*

source of inflation in all three countries is deficit spending. They consider the logic of cause and effect to be indisputable: Paying off debt by increasing the amount of currency circulating in an economy, without increasing production, inevitably leads to higher prices.

"Inflation is always and everywhere a monetary phenomenon."
— *Milton Friedman, 1970*

Growth in a nation's money supply allows prices to go up, fueling inflation as a result. As Exhibit 2 shows, the quantity of currency in Brazil, Argentina and Bolivia has skyrocketed since 1980, the same period when inflation shot through the roof in all three countries.

As currency supplies grew in these South American countries, deficit spending reached mammoth proportions:

- In 1985, just before Bolivia reached record inflation levels of 50,000 percent annualized, its tax revenues covered just 15 percent of government expenditures. Total government revenues were only 1.3 percent of the gross domestic product for the first half of 1985.

- Argentina's deficit reached 11 percent of its gross domestic product in 1985, resulting in an annual inflation rate of about 1,000 percent. It is estimated that Argentina collects only 1.6 percent of the personal income taxes it is due.

- In 1988, after three consecutive years of increasing its money supply by over 300 percent while amassing debt equal to one-third its GDP, Brazil had nearly 1,000 percent inflation.

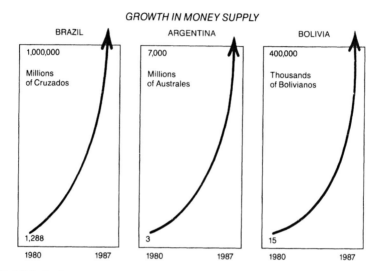

GROWTH IN MONEY SUPPLY

BRAZIL — 1,000,000 / Millions of Cruzados / 1,288 / 1980 – 1987

ARGENTINA — 7,000 / Millions of Australes / 3 / 1980 – 1987

BOLIVIA — 400,000 / Thousands of Bolivianos / 15 / 1980 – 1987

Exhibit 2: *Brazil, Argentina and Bolivia drove their economies toward hyperinflation by printing huge quantities of money since 1980. Brazil, for example, had the equivalent of only 1.288 billion cruzados in 1980, but increased that almost 100-fold to over one trillion cruzados by 1987. (All three countries have adopted new currencies since 1985. Both Brazil and Argentina lopped three zeros off their currencies, renaming them the cruzado and the austral, respectively. Bolivia took the extreme step of lopping off six zeros in renaming its currency the boliviano. Money supply figures for 1980 are the equivalent in today's currency of the currency used in 1980.)*

Brazil and Argentina are still struggling with intolerably high inflation rates, finishing 1988 at 934 percent in Brazil and 376 percent in Argentina. Though Bolivia has temporarily reduced its inflation to about 20 percent, it has done so at tremendous cost: its economy is now operating far below capacity, with extremely high rates of unemployment.

It is easy to dismiss the relevance of South American economic experiences because of the relative weakness of these nations, but to do so is to underestimate both the economies in question and the devastating impact of severe inflation.

Brazil, for example, boasts the eighth largest economy in the world, and the sixth largest population. It is among the world's leading arms and small aircraft manufacturers, is second only to the U.S. in total food exports, and leads the world in orange juice exports. Because of the size and youth of its population (over half its 140 million people are under 20), Brazil also has the potential to play an even larger role in the world's future economy.

Argentina, on the other hand, is a prime example of a once mighty economy demolished by runaway inflation. From the early 1900s until about 1950 it was a global economic power. Unhindered by massive deficit spending, Argentina was once the fifth most productive nation in the world. Today, its gross domestic product ranks seventeenth.

Inflation has devastated the currencies of all three countries in the world market. As Exhibit 3 illustrates, the value of Brazilian, Argentine and Bolivian currencies has plummeted on the international exchange market.

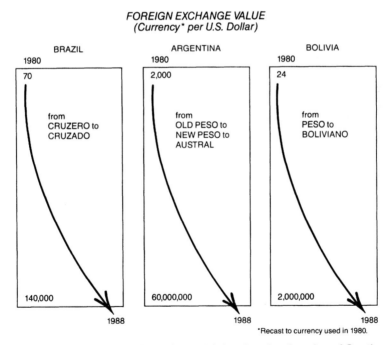

FOREIGN EXCHANGE VALUE
(Currency* per U.S. Dollar)

*Recast to currency used in 1980.

Exhibit 3: These charts show the rapid deterioration in value of South American currencies — specifically in relation to the U.S. dollar — as a result of hyperinflation. For example, in Bolivia, it took only 24 pesos to buy a dollar in 1980. In 1985, the near-worthless peso was replaced by the boliviano, and by 1988 it took the equivalent of over two million pesos to buy a single dollar.

The U.S. Follows South America's Path to Hyperinflation

South American executives warn that, just as it is a mistake to dismiss the lessons offered by their crumbling economies, it is extremely dangerous to underestimate America's vulnerability to inflation.

Among economists, business executives and banking officials in Argentina, Brazil and Bolivia, there is widespread agreement that the United States government is following the same path their governments followed, plunging head-on toward runaway inflation.

There is also considerable surprise that Americans do not seem to see the disastrous possibility they face. As evidence that America is well along the road to high inflation rates, South Americans point to several factors the U.S. has in common with their pre-hyperinflationary economies:

- Large deficits.
- Deterioration in our international balance of payments.
- Calls for protectionism.
- Eroded confidence in our national currency.
- Our currency's declining international exchange value.

Exhibit 4 depicts the climbing U.S. budget and trade deficits, and the dollar's falling international exchange value.

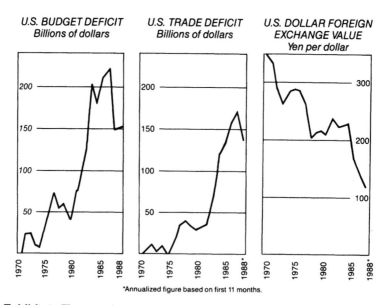

Exhibit 4: *The steady increase in U.S. budget and trade deficits has corresponded with a precipitous drop in the dollar's international exchange value. This situation is similar to that found in Brazil, Argentina and Bolivia over the past decade.*

Of course, this does not mean the United States will inevitably face the triple-digit inflation experienced by Argentina, Bolivia and Brazil. However, it certainly suggests a strong prospect of rising inflation rates, and South American executives warn it would not take triple-digit inflation to devastate the American economy. Even a diluted version of South America's inflationary experience would have terrible repercussions here, because, according to many South Americans, it is not so much the level of inflation that is difficult to live with as it is the fluctuation in rates.

Argentina, for example, learned to cope with 100 percent annual inflation, but a fivefold increase to 500 percent plunged the country into chaos.

Likewise, 5 percent may be tolerable in the United States, but a sudden fivefold increase to 25 percent would profoundly change our economic realities. As a matter of fact, when President Nixon took the extraordinary step of instituting wage and price controls in 1971, inflation was *only 4.7 percent.*

Preparing for Hyperinflation, U.S.A.

It is doubtful that there are executives in any other part of the world who can match the South Americans as far as modern inflation-fighting experience. They have operated for decades in the face of some of the highest peacetime inflation rates in history. Indeed, many have never known any other environment. As one Argentine banker said, "I'm 42 years old, and I can't imagine what life would be like without inflation." The lessons these business, banking and economic leaders offer can be immensely valuable for their American counterparts, and can help U.S. business managers prepare for an uncertain future in which they, too, may face rapidly rising prices and towering interest rates.

Admittedly, the business climates of Argentina, Bolivia and Brazil are not identical to that of the United States. Many of the techniques used throughout South America in fighting inflation are at odds with either American laws or customs. For example, many individuals and businesses in South America admit they don't pay taxes, and wonder why anyone would. Still, many inflation-coping methods apply to the U.S.

Hyperinflation Requires Hypermanagement

While many of the management practices undertaken during hyperinflation are also common in stable economic environments, during hyperinflation they become much more critical. Whereas American managers currently have time to consider, plan and discuss their responses to problems and opportunities, the constant change and instability of high inflation creates an ongoing crisis that demands immediate and continual reaction by management. Under such circumstances, the impact of small errors can be greatly magnified.

Should the United States enter a period of high inflation, those companies not prepared to make drastic adjustments will probably not exist for long.

Operating a company in a hyperinflationary environment can be a nightmare. There is absolutely no stability, and the cost of doing business is mercurial. Salaries escalate almost daily, the price of key raw materials can skyrocket from one day to the next, and supplies often dry up overnight.

While good management skills are a prerequisite for success in any business climate, during hyperinflation they are an absolute requirement for survival. Well-managed companies can maintain stability under chaotic conditions, and many even earn healthy profits. Conversely, bad management practices are magnified during hyperinflation, both because of the continual need for instant decisions and the thin line between survival and disaster. Hyperinflation has driven many poorly managed companies to an early grave, some plummeting from solvency to bankruptcy in a period of weeks.

Because events occur so rapidly during hyperinflation, those companies that can maintain their flexibility are best off. New information must be absorbed quickly, and today's political or monetary event can negate yesterday's wise business decision, requiring an immediate change of course. In many instances, a one-day delay in making or implementing a decision can be devastating. At some point, though, flexibility itself can create additional chaos, so it is necessary to implement a wide range of checks and balances, and at all times bear in mind that a single error can be fatal.

The key to operating in a hyperinflationary economy is to stay ever mindful that the real value of money erodes significantly over very short periods of time. Any aspect of management that involves cash transactions takes on added urgency, which gives the chief financial officer a major role in almost all day-to-day decisions. Cash management becomes the most critical component of business operation, and the difference between profitability and bankruptcy is often simply a matter of how well a firm handles its cash.

In any sale, the payment price begins to lose its value before the ink on the invoice is dry, and any delay in collecting payment will result in a lower real price. At 20 percent monthly inflation — Brazil's 1988 average — a 30-day delay can wipe out the better part of a product's profit margin, and two months can make the sale a money-loser.

Prices are increased rapidly during high inflation, and payment is collected as soon as possible and invested immediately upon receipt. Cash is never left idle — investments are made overnight and renewed daily, because the value of money can trickle to nothing if it fails to earn sufficient interest to keep step with inflation.

Likewise, any delay in purchasing supplies will result in higher costs, and South Americans routinely stockpile huge amounts of inventory to avoid price increases.

Production Plays a Smaller Role in Survival

High inflation changes the fundamental texture of business operation, and can even alter the focus of individual businesses. Operating an efficient company often takes a back seat to money management, and some companies allow their manufacturing operations to grind to a virtual halt. Product lines that may once

have been a staple of business can suddenly become unprofitable, and have to be abandoned.

Managers turn from production and long-term planning to financial arbitrage, surviving by speculating in the currency and commodities markets. Many South American companies invest their money in other countries, or at least place their assets in a more stable currency, most often the U.S. dollar. South American companies also commonly stockpile large inventories as a speculative device, with expectations of selling them later at substantially higher prices.

Other South American companies cope with hyperinflation through a strategy of vertical integration. By acquiring raw materials and production and distribution facilities, some corporations have been able to minimize the impact of price fluctuations and government regulations.

There are no long-term, fixed-price contracts. At Bolivia's 1985 inflationary peak, all payments had to be in cash at the prevailing black market rate. If not in cash, all payments are indexed, so that the bill goes up over time according to an inflationary index, to ensure that the value of the payment does not decrease in real terms.

The Great Credit Drought

During hyperinflation, loans are available only for short periods, and at extremely high interest rates. Cash becomes the nearly universal medium of exchange, and capital expenditures are often sacrificed for the sake of survival.

Because credit is so tight and interest rates so high, the relationship between a business and its bankers and investors often changes. Companies are forced to widen their circle of creditors to improve the availability of capital.

Businesses cannot afford to be heavily leveraged since interest rates are so unpredictable. Imagine those Brazilian firms that made an investment decision based on the 70 percent annual interest rates prevailing in November 1986, and then found themselves faced with an actual interest rate of 550 percent only 90 days later. Such instability is enough to ruin even the best laid plans.

Personnel needs often change during hyperinflation, requiring larger accounting and data-processing staffs. The labor/management relationship also tends to become more adversarial, because of the constant demand for wage hikes and the ever-present threat of layoffs. In addition, the relationship between management layers can become more tense, as middle management is generally hardest hit by inflation.

Filling supply needs is a much more complex process during hyperinflation. The number of sources for any given product tends to dwindle, so competition is often nonexistent. Suppliers frequently sit on their goods in anticipation of price increases, and in some cases demand immediate payment in cash. There is much less tolerance for overdue debts. At the same time, companies may attempt to stockpile inventories, both to ensure future supplies and as a speculative device.

A consistent, reliable source of raw materials and parts is of course critical to all companies, but particularly those operating in a hyperinflationary economy, since they tend to be mired in regulations and controls which can cause local supply sources to disappear.

High inflation can also affect the relative affordability and availability of foreign supplies and sales, especially when protectionist legislation is enacted, as it often is. Manufacturers who rely on imported parts may have an especially difficult time obtaining or affording those parts.

Fluid Management Style a Must

Reporting structures and managerial authority also undergo transformations as inflation rises. Because decisions have to be made quickly, there is no time for red tape or chain-of-command approval processes. Managers on every level must understand financial management, corporate objectives and rules, and must be given the authority to act quickly and independently. Likewise, they must communicate verbally, because the time involved in communicating via written messages is simply too valuable to waste.

Information, always important, is absolutely critical during hyperinflation. It is crucial not only that a company understand the true impact inflation is having on its costs and operations, but also that it develop the ability to gather and use information to predict future costs. This requires that businesses monitor the government, competitors, financial markets, the foreign exchange, and even black markets, and that they attempt, whenever possible, to anticipate changes in any of these spheres.

Governments also tend to play a larger role when inflation rises, as regulations — especially wage and price controls — are routinely introduced in an attempt to keep inflation down. And, as regulations are introduced, the temptation to circumvent them builds, especially when companies aren't allowed to pass on higher costs in the form of price increases. Inevitably, price controls lead to shortages, which in turn lead to black markets.

During hyperinflation, companies become extremely vulnerable to corruption. Some of the smaller South American companies have gone so far as to put family members in key positions inside the company to protect themselves from employee theft. Short-cutting regulations becomes all-pervasive, and everyone plays the black market.

The immediate need to survive begins to dominate all business decisions and behavior, making long-term planning a rare and generally futile exercise. Events simply change too fast and too unpredictably. During hyperinflation, the outlook of a long-term plan may be reduced to a few weeks, whereas short-term may cover only a few days.

Hyperinflation Is Immune to Politics

History has shown again and again that once hyperinflation becomes a reality, politicians inevitably succumb to the temptation of trying to legislate it out of existence, and just as inevitably fail. This was the case after both World War I and World War II in Europe, and more recently in Argentina, Bolivia and Brazil, each of which has imposed wage and price controls in the past decade.

These controls succeeded only in disrupting natural market forces of supply and demand, and usually led to shortages of basic commodities, hoarding, black markets and devious wage and pricing practices.

We must also remember that, as recently as 1971, the U.S. government imposed wage and price controls, and these measures proved to be as unsuccessful in the United States as they have been in South America.

In South America, government restrictions resulted in an increase in white collar crime, as a never-ending cycle developed in which the government implemented a maze of regulations, and citizens and companies just as quickly found some way to evade them.

Hyperinflation is by no means a certainty for the United States, but we have managed to create conditions conducive to its development, not the least of which is our widespread refusal to believe that it can happen here. According to several South American executives, not only can runaway inflation happen in the U.S., but it can easily catch the nation off guard, plodding along unnoticed before heading upward suddenly and without warning into the region of ruinous rates.

Granted that the U.S. economy and political structure are much more stable and powerful — and much less prone to chaos — than those of any South American country, but the parallels remain. And, more importantly, no country anywhere, during any time in world history, has been able to survive over a prolonged period by spending money at a faster clip than it takes it in.

"Do not accustom yourself to consider debt as only an inconvenience. You will find it a calamity."
— Samuel Johnson, 1758

The intention of this manual is not to predict future U.S. inflationary trends. Rather, it is meant to provide information that will allow American businesses to fare as well as possible should inflation begin to rise in America, as so many world business and political leaders fear it will.

If inflation does take off here, the lessons of South Americans who have successfully battled its ravages can help ensure that American business will land on its feet.

FÉLIX DE BARRIO

Buenos Aires, January 8, 1987

Mr. Harry E. Figgie, Jr.
FIGGIE INTERNATIONAL
1000 Virginia Center Parkway
Richmond, Virginia 23295
U. S. A.

Dear Mr. Figgie,

Yesterday I had a very pleasant meeting with Mr. Gerald J. Swanson talking about the realities of inflation in countries such as Argentina. Mr. Swanson left me a copy of your 1985 Annual Report which is the first down-to-earth one I have seen coming from a U.S. corporation.

The Perspective Column you have written, could just as well have been written by me - if I had the talent, that is -. So many times in the last few years I have argued with U.S. citizens about the incredible mistakes being made in U.S. economy, and so few times I had anybody agreeing !

Historically all countries that ruled the world sooner or later started on the downhill slope. It looks as if your politicians want the U.S. to follow the pattern. But after reading your column I see why. The U.S. was on the way up when everybody said "I am an American". The U.S. is on its way down since individuals and politicians care first for themselves, second for their party and only in third instance for their country. Unfortunately this is exactly what has happened in Argentina for the last 40 to 50 years. And look where we are now.

I also enjoyed tremendously your letter to the stockholders. It is a pleasant surprise to see for once a conglomerate that does not dump companies as soon as they have a bad year. So many "executives" live and swear by the immediate result! And this is why U.S. industry is falling behind Japan and Germany, where the future of the company has precedence over executives' yearly bonuses.

Congratulations Mr. Figgie for a job well done.

Very sincerely,

Félix de Barrio

14

1

Financial Management

*"Inflation is when you go to the same
restaurant each morning, order the same
breakfast, and each time have to ask how
much it costs."*
— *Brazilian businessman*

The critical factor that distinguishes the financial management of a business under high inflation is the two-dimensional nature of money. Because of the speed with which the buying power of cash erodes, its value is a matter not just of quantity, but of timing — when it is invested, when it is received, when it is paid out, etc.

Under such circumstances, any monetary transaction takes on a much greater immediacy. A dollar today is quite literally not a dollar tomorrow, and the value of a corporation's cash holdings and receivables deteriorates rapidly. As a result, the precise timing of any transaction can become as important — or even more so — than the specific amount involved.

While cash management is an important aspect of business management in any economy, it is absolutely critical during hyperinflation. For many South American companies, intelligent, innovative cash management provides a major source of corporate profits. Likewise, poor cash management has destroyed companies throughout South America with a speed that is unrivaled in the American business arena.

The impact of money's increased two-dimensional nature is broad, changing the very way business managers must look at their operations. Cash management becomes the primary key to success and failure, shifting the relative importance of the various departments of a business. Hyperinflation changes not only the pace at which decisions must be made, but the ways in which they are made, and it alters a business's relationship with constituents ranging from its customers and suppliers to its banks and investors.

Among all the factors that arise for businesses facing high inflation rates, there is none more important than the impact of time on money.

■ *Make absolutely certain your managers understand the time value of money.*

Management from top to bottom must be aware of the time value of money, because it is a critical consideration in any decision involving a financial transaction. Failure to consider the impact of time into such decisions can be ruinous.

One area where time is particularly important is purchasing, because a delay in ordering and/or paying for inventory can significantly increase a company's costs. In Brazil during early 1988, it took less than four months for the average item to double in price.

Time is perhaps an even more critical factor when making a sale. In the United States, terms of sale might include a discount for a payment made in ten days, or the full amount if payment is made in thirty days. This would be disastrous in a hyperinflationary economy, where, at the extreme, a thirty-day delay could cut the value received for a product in half. Even waiting as little as seven days is a big mistake unless interest that reflects the rate of inflation is charged for every day's delay.

In South America, this is particularly problematic when dealing with government agencies, which are notoriously late in their payments. Since the state owns and operates such a large percentage of the economy, this can be a serious problem for private suppliers. When not restricted by wage and price controls, firms compensate for these delays by adding an extra margin into the prices they charge the government.

While the government may not be a problematic customer in the United States, certain other buyers might. Firms may want to analyze the payment histories of their customers to determine those who tend to drag out their payables, and charge these customers a premium to counteract the lessened value of late payments.

■ *Never allow your cash to remain idle.*

All South American companies share one common bit of philosophy: Never leave cash so that it is not earning interest, even for one day. Cash investments are made on an overnight basis and renewed daily.

Payment for goods and services is received as quickly as possible, and then that payment is used immediately. It is either invested in a high-yield money market account, used to purchase some kind of hard goods or inventory, or placed into a dollar-denominated account, which often means it is sent out of the country.

Since rates vary among different banks, it is not unusual for a firm's financial officer to call many banks at the end of each business day in search of the best overnight rate. Available cash is then spread between three or four banks for security, in case one bank goes bankrupt.

Many South American companies with excess cash choose to lend it to others. High reserve requirements, as much as 90 percent of deposits, make it difficult for South American banks to meet the financial needs of local corporations. Successful companies with surplus cash often fill this void by becoming competitors of the local banking establishment, and many generate significant interest income.

While every company may employ any of a variety of cash investment options during hyperinflation, every successful company has one policy in common: cash is *never* left idle.

■ *Good cash management can provide a major source of profit, while poor cash management can destroy a company in a matter of months.*

In hyperinflation, operational management frequently takes a back seat to cash management, which can have an immense impact on a firm's income. The earned interest on the lending and investing of surplus cash can become an important ingredient in a company's total profits.

In 1985, one client of a large Argentine public accounting firm earned more than half its $200 million pretax income from investing the company's cash. The following year, another Argentine manufacturer's interest income accounted for $47 million of its $103 million profit. These figures are not at all unusual in a hyperinflationary economy, but would be inordinately high for a U.S. manufacturing firm.

Rarely does interest income have a significant impact on the profits of an American manufacturer.

By the same token, many South American businessmen and bankers indicate that, during high inflation, poor cash management can destroy a company within months, if not weeks. If cash is allowed to stay idle without earning interest income — if cash is not earning interest at all times, or customers are allowed to drag out payables without being charged a premium to counteract inflation — the firm's asset balance and profits will be reduced and may over time be wiped out altogether.

■ *Be prepared to convert dollars into a stable foreign currency.*

Should inflation accelerate in the United States, American businesses may be forced to convert their dollar holdings into a more stable currency to keep the value of their assets from plummeting.

Throughout Brazil, Argentina and Bolivia, companies routinely hold a minimal proportion of their money in domestic currencies, converting the remainder into a more stable currency whenever possible. Most often they turn to the U.S. dollar.

American businesses facing runaway inflation will have to seek an alternative currency. This may be the German mark, Swiss franc, Japanese yen or some other currency, depending on conditions in foreign exchange markets at the time.

This conversion may be significantly more difficult for American businesses than it is for South American businesses. The dollar is currently the world's most freely traded currency, and Brazil, Argentina and Bolivia have developed domestic exchange markets based on the dollar, institutionalizing its existence in their economies. The U.S. has no such system in place for a second currency, and access to an alternative currency may be limited.

■ *Whenever possible, deal in cash payments.*

Businessmen have to be very careful in extending credit during hyperinflation, so it is always safest to complete deals immediately, in cash. Indexation — the normal alternative to cash payment — is not a cure-all, and no index accurately reflects the individual seller's own inflation rate. While every company has its own specific mix of necessary resources, indexes are based on averages, and may or may not be favorable to the companies in question.

In Bolivia in 1985, during the worst of that country's hyperinflationary crisis, terms of sale generally dictated that the price charged for goods was the price in effect at the time the customer received the merchandise. All payments had to be made in cash, and the price was determined not by using the official currency exchange rate, but by using the black market currency exchange rate, which more accurately reflected the inflationary impact on the value of the currency than did the official rate.

■ *Anticipate competition between the buyer and seller over when payments will be made.*

The timing of payments takes on added importance during hyperinflation, and the issue of who is going to have the use of the money and when it will be available may be a key negotiating point between buyer and seller.

A seller that is in desperate need of cash may give a buyer a significant price discount for early cash payment. Buyers, on the other hand, may try to negotiate long lags in payment schedules in order to assure their own access to cash, and may be willing to pay a significantly higher price for a longer payment schedule.

■ *Work continually to maintain positive real interest rates.*

Because of the volatility of real interest rates during hyperinflation, the interest rates firms charge on their own receivables can result in substantial gains or losses.

When establishing the interest rates due on receivables, firms in South America tend to factor in the highest projected inflation rate at the time the price is established. When inflation rates are lower than anticipated, high positive interest rates — or rates greater than the inflation rate — are realized, often resulting in substantial windfall profits.

The opposite — ruinous losses — can result if a company establishes an interest rate that is lower than the actual inflation rate — or a negative real interest rate.

Very often, South American governments set negative interest rates while trying not to admit the depth of their inflationary problems. This policy puts pressure on companies to maintain an interest rate in line with the established government interest rate.

During the 1970s, savings and loans in the United States found themselves in a financial squeeze because many of the home mortgages they had outstanding yielded a negative interest rate. Meanwhile, they were forced to pay their depositors a positive interest rate that was adjusted for the high rates of inflation. American companies should be careful not to allow themselves to be placed in a similar squeeze should inflation rates take off.

■ *Develop practices that enable you to internally finance working capital.*

Private companies within Bolivia, Brazil and Argentina are extremely limited in their efforts to borrow money, and it is a fair assumption that a similar condition would develop in the United States if inflation rises sufficiently.

According to the South American model, banks have very small amounts of money to lend during high inflation, and the money they do have is made available only at extremely high interest rates and only for short periods of time. In the first quarter of 1988, for example, companies needing capital in Brazil had to pay 15 to 18 percent monthly interest on loans. (The cost of a loan at such rates is shown in Exhibit 5.)

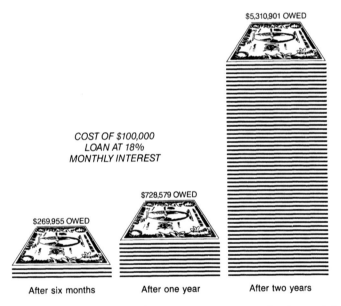

$5,310,901 OWED

COST OF $100,000
LOAN AT 18%
MONTHLY INTEREST

$728,579 OWED

$269,955 OWED

After six months   After one year   After two years

Exhibit 5: *The compounding of interest rates commonly charged during hyperinflation can make loans astronomically expensive. At 18 percent monthly interest, a $100,000 loan would cost over $5 million if left unpaid for just two years.*

During hyperinflation, venture capital is not really an alternative either, since available funds can instead be invested in bonds with an extremely high yield, and much of the money leaves the country for safer, more certain investments.

Often a company's only choice is to borrow from its parent company outside the country, or, as is most often the case, not to borrow at all. This inability to borrow results in a stagnation of investments and a severe curtailment of economic growth.

Most companies, therefore, can expand only through internal financing, and working capital needs are typically met by customers.

In Brazil, for example, purchasers of capital equipment pay as much as 50 percent down, with the balance to be adjusted by indexation. Each sale is treated differently, and the amount of down payment depends on the financial condition of the customer, and its relationship to the supplier. In some extreme cases, sales are strictly in cash, and many South American companies go so far as to negotiate with their customers for prepayment of orders.

■ Consider the possibility of acting as an acceptance company to facilitate your customers' purchases.

The evaporation of capital during high inflation often leaves customers unable to finance their own needs. Because of this, companies may be forced to consider financing their customers' purchases. Though there is high risk to extending credit in high inflationary periods, acting as an acceptance company may be the only way to maintain sales, and can generate additional profits if positive interest rates are maintained.

During Bolivia's 1985 hyperinflationary crisis, for example, most of the customers of a distributor of construction equipment were unable to obtain bank financing. In order to survive, the distributor was forced to step in and finance the purchases itself.

The inability of customers to borrow money for purchases can also be overcome by leasing agreements. For example, after an in-depth analysis of its sales network, a leading multinational manufacturer found that most of its customers and potential customers in Argentina were unable to obtain financing to purchase its product. As a result, the company was losing sales to a competitor that offered its customers an inferior product but better financial terms. The multinational, not wanting to establish an acceptance company, decided the best method to maintain sales was to lease rather than sell its product. Rentals became a form of lending, with the lease contracts tied to the exchange rate between the U.S. dollar and the Argentine austral. Through this innovative method of making its product more accessible, the company protected itself against inflation and its business soared.

It is important to note that in a hyperinflationary economy, overcoming your customers' inability to obtain financing is often as important a selling tool as product quality or price. Salesmen are often required to sell not only a product, but also a method to finance purchase of that product.

■ *Make the rapid collection of receivables a primary goal.*

Because money loses its value so quickly and working capital is in such short supply during hyperinflation, the timely collection of receivables becomes absolutely critical. It is also important that, immediately upon receipt, all payments are deposited in interest-bearing accounts.

The fact that tomorrow's money will be worth significantly less than what it is worth today is perhaps the single most important lesson to remember about surviving hyperinflation. A delay in receiving payment of as little as a week, surely a month, without a premium to reflect inflation, can completely eliminate your profit margin, and may well place a company in a loss position from which it might never recover. (Exhibit 6 shows how rapidly the value of receivables erodes when they are past due.)

The reason is simple. In Brazil, for example, at 18 percent monthly inflation, if you are owed 10,000 cruzados on January 1 but don't receive the money until February 1, the payment will only be worth the equivalent of 8,200 cruzados. By March 1, it will be worth only 6,724 cruzados. A 30 percent profit margin — fairly good by American standards — would have totally disappeared during this two-month period.

In Argentina, Bolivia and Brazil, one of a business's most important goals is to keep its DSO (days sales outstanding) as low as possible. Large firms sometimes use their leverage to force rapid payment from their customers, using their size to delay their own payments to their creditors at the same time. This is an obvious attempt to beat inflation at both ends of the spectrum — when paying *and* collecting bills.

Because of the high time value of money, South American companies often penalize those customers who do not pay promptly. These slow-paying buyers are often the last to have their orders filled, and their new orders are frequently rejected. This becomes particularly critical as shortages develop, a typical occurrence once governments attempt to halt hyperinflation through wage and price controls.

DECREASING VALUE OF OVERDUE RECEIVABLES
At 18% monthly inflation

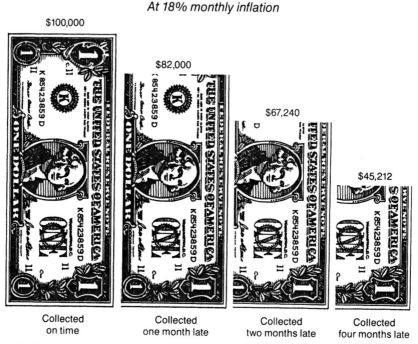

$100,000 — Collected on time

$82,000 — Collected one month late

$67,240 — Collected two months late

$45,212 — Collected four months late

Exhibit 6: *With inflation running 18 percent monthly, a $100,000 payment will lose more than half its purchasing power if it is collected just four months late.*

■ *Be aware that the stock market may become an uncertain source of capital.*

The ability of the government to control inflation greatly influences the stability of the stock market. In inflationary economies, like those in South America, stock markets tend to resemble roller coasters, in which peaks and valleys in stock prices correspond to hopes of economic reform and fears of economic collapse.

As inflation rises, investors often abandon the stock market, making it significantly less useful as a source of capital.

Brazil's stock market, the largest in any developing country, provides an excellent illustration of the volatility brought on by inflation. In February 1986, the Brazilian stock market soared on hopes surrounding the Cruzado Plan, which the government introduced to curb the inflationary spiral. From February 1986 to

April 1986, the Bovespa Index — similar to the U.S. Dow Jones Average — more than doubled. Then the Cruzado Plan began to falter, price freezes caused company profits to disappear, and, between April 1986 and October 1986, the Index declined 50 percent.

The stock market does well during early stages of a new plan to control inflation because individuals react negatively to the lower interest rates banks pay as the inflation rate falls. Depositors tend to withdraw their money from banks in favor of investments they believe will yield a higher rate of return, such as the stock market or properties. As inflation begins to build again, interest rates increase, and fears about economic stability grow, driving many investors to desert the stock market and deposit in banks again.

If inflation rises in the U.S., firms should anticipate a flight of capital — particularly foreign capital — from our stock market. This may limit the market's viability as a source of equity capital, making it more difficult for companies to raise money. Domestic investors as well as foreign investors will seek safer havens for their funds, and will tend to turn their backs on the stock market.

In Brazil, where 3,400 companies are qualified to issue stock, only 610 companies were traded on the market in 1986. The rest chose not to enter the market at all because it was an uncertain source of capital.

The U.S. stock market may be hit especially hard by inflation because of the huge role foreign investors play here. When a country experiences inflation, foreigners tend to become very leary of investing in its stock market because they face a double risk: first, that the currency will devalue, reducing the value of stock holdings; and second, that the market will plunge because of economic instability. These two events can lead to a double loss for the foreign investor.

If inflation rises in the United States, then, it is likely that many investors will flee the stock market, substantially reducing its usefulness as a source of capital.

■ Develop relationships with several banks to facilitate capital availability in tightened capital markets.

Banks play an integral role in a company's operation during hyperinflation, and under such conditions it may become necessary to develop or maintain relationships with more than one bank. Some companies in South America have deposits with as many as 17.

Because access to capital during high inflation is extremely limited, a connection with several lending institutions increases a firm's chances of obtaining financing when necessary. The more banks a company does business with, the more potential sources of credit it has.

As mentioned earlier, another reason South American companies deal with several banks is the increased rate of bank failures during high inflation. By spreading their deposits around, companies avoid risking too much with any single institution.

A third reason to conduct business with numerous banks is to have branches in a wide variety of locations. Since every hour counts, one can't afford the lost time that would result in having checks sent to a central location and then deposited. A five-day lag in the deposit could significantly reduce the value of the payment. In Brazil, for example, most customers pay their invoices directly to a bank rather than to the company itself, postal boxes, or lock boxes.

Problems related to the timeliness of bank transactions are unlikely to be so great in the United States because of the increasingly widespread use of electronic fund transfers. Should inflation begin to take off here, it is likely this trend will accelerate.

■ Make corresponding accounts and tax deposits a key negotiating point with your banks.

Much more than in the United States, South American companies constantly negotiate with their banks to obtain better financial arrangements. One reason they do so is because during hyperinflation, the interest income available to banks in corresponding accounts and tax deposits is substantial, and can often be used for leverage in these negotiations.

In Brazil, for example, businesses are required to deposit payroll taxes three days after paying an employee, but banks have ten days to deposit that money with the government. During hyperinflation, this seven-day difference can mean substantial earnings for the bank. At one point in 1987, the annualized interest rate stood at 900 percent, or approximately 2½ percent a day in simple interest. On a deposit of $1 million, that seven-day delay would net the bank approximately $175,000.

With such sums at stake, management is well-advised to negotiate with several different banks to determine where it can receive the most favorable terms. Often, companies expect a share of this windfall. In some cases, they share in the interest earned on the tax deposit, and in others they receive special banking services at no extra charge. Among the services a bank might offer a company is a computer linkage that will provide instant cash balance information, which is critical because effective money management, and therefore the profitability of a firm, depends on responding to events quickly and making certain that all available funds are invested at the best possible rate.

■ *Develop your ability to anticipate changes in monetary and fiscal policy and the effects on interest rates in financial markets.*

It is always vital for chief financial officers to have comprehensive, up-to-date information concerning where money can be invested most profitably, but during hyperinflation, information becomes dated with incredible speed, and its timeliness and accuracy can have an immense impact on a company's profits. Operation during times of rapid change requires increased attention to the government's economic policies, because changes in these policies can have major effects on a firm's profitability over very short periods of time.

"In an effort to put a lid on inflation, Congress today voted to move the decimal point one digit to the left."

In South America, knowledge of a change in monetary policy, government bond rates, or the size of a bond issue are all eagerly awaited by businessmen and individuals alike. Getting the jump on officially released information by as little as five minutes can be extremely profitable. Those people with access to government officials have a tremendous advantage in determining how their cash should be used.

Gathering and acting on such information can be the key to survival, and often takes precedence over standard operational concerns. According to a Bolivian banker, during the worst of that country's hyperinflationary crisis, "No company survived by doing what it was supposed to do. Everyone speculated."

Regardless of how detailed or up-to-the-minute one's information is, there is always a high degree of uncertainty when making decisions in a high inflationary economy because of the rate at which all economic factors change. One can never be sure that economic data is being interpreted correctly. Prices and rates rise so rapidly that even the best laid plans can go suddenly and disastrously awry.

During one particularly volatile month in early 1987, the president of a Brazilian manufacturer of healthcare products was faced with the decision of putting his company's excess cash back into his company, or into a ninety-day money market account. In one form or another, thousands of South American businessmen are confronted with this kind of decision every day. In this case, since the government had recently forced up interest rates to discourage borrowing for the purpose of speculating on raw materials, this Brazilian executive chose a 90-day account paying 300 percent annual interest. A week later, the government decided to tighten credit further and interest rates jumped to 400 percent, turning the executive's well-reasoned decision into an unfortunate one. By locking in his money just one week too early, he forfeited 20 percent in interest earnings. On a $100,000 investment, that would translate into a loss of over $8,000 in just 90 days.

Because interest rates become so volatile, hyperinflation is a second-guesser's breeding ground.

■ *Be prepared to maintain more than one set of books.*

During hyperinflation, historical costs become meaningless as a means of comparison, and multiple sets of books are necessary to get an accurate picture of performance.

Consider what would happen to an Argentine company that simply kept a single set of books in australes. It might double its profits from one million to two million australes between 1986 and 1987, but the failure to understand what that means in real terms would be ruinous. While one million australes were worth $795,545 on December 31, 1986, a year later two million australes were worth only $533,333. In this hypothetical case, an apparent 100 percent increase in profits was a 33 percent decrease in real terms.

To combat this problem, virtually every company in Argentina, Bolivia and Brazil keeps more than one set of books, and some companies keep as many as four. This obviously increases the number of individuals required in an accounting department. Several South American financial directors reported that they had to double their staffs to cope with the requirements of inflationary bookkeeping.

In Argentina, for example, one set of books is kept in australes, the new Argentine currency. In order to make historical comparisons to past years, another set is maintained in pesos, the old currency. A third set is maintained in U.S. dollars. This is often the set that is used to manage the company, and is the one that is always used by U.S. multinationals, since SEC regulations mandate that they must report in a manner consistent with their U.S. parent. Finally, there is a concept in vogue among some companies to keep a set of books in units of the products they produce. In this way, they eliminate any inflationary impact on their operations by tracking sales growth in physical units sold rather than sales revenue.

Because of the necessity of maintaining different sets of books in different currencies, the preparation of financial statements is terribly confusing. Firms have to develop systems that provide current information in such areas as prices, costs and inventories. They need a financial system and reporting structure that will reflect inflation's overall impact on the performance of their business and allow them to make informed decisions. These systems should have the capability of being updated on a daily basis so that they reflect the most current price changes taking place in the economy.

Such systems will be more easily developed in the United States than in South America because of the greater prevalence of computerized information processing here. American firms preparing for high inflation would be wise to ensure that their computer capabilities are sophisticated enough to perform the necessary functions.

■ *Inventory valuation should be based on NIFO rather than LIFO.*

Another difficulty of maintaining accurate financial records in an inflationary economy is the valuation of inventory. The standard inventory valuation practice in the United States is LIFO, or Last In First Out. LIFO assumes that items purchased last will be sold first. By valuating inventory items at the price of the most recent purchases, inventory value becomes comparable to current prices.

In South America, on the other hand, the inventory valuation process is taken one step further by the use of NIFO, or Next In First Out. NIFO is used to reflect future inflation by valuing the cost of replacing inventory. NIFO valuation is, in effect, a company's best guess as to the impact of the future rate of inflation on the costs of the materials it uses.

If a company were to use LIFO during high inflationary periods, it would be greatly underpricing the value of its inventory and therefore eroding its profit margin. At Brazil's current 20 percent monthly inflation rate, an inventory valuated at $1 million with LIFO would have an actual replacement cost of $1,200,000 after just one month. In such a case, NIFO would have avoided a potential $200,000 undervaluation of inventory.

■ *Develop an appropriate inflationary adjustment for capital replacement or the value of your capital will disappear.*

Tax depreciation deductions are normally based on original purchase costs rather than replacement costs. However, high inflation has a major impact on a firm's capital replacement costs and failure to take this into account during such times can be suicidal, because it can cause the firm's capital base to disappear.

For example, if a Brazilian company purchases a piece of equipment for 300,000 cruzados, it might be allowed to deduct

100,000 per year from its taxable income for three years. But at 400 percent per year inflation, the replacement cost three years later would be more in the neighborhood of 37,500,000 cruzados. Unless the company increases its annual depreciation to account for this inflationary effect, the value of its capital stock for tax purposes will decline to virtually zero.

Under such circumstances, inflation will not only eliminate a company's ability to recapture its capital base, but will also cause the firm to have virtually no depreciation deductions for tax purposes.

The inability of a country's businesses to recapture the true cost of their capital will obviously have a very negative impact on capital formation within the country as a whole.

SUMMARY

- Make absolutely certain your managers understand the time value of money.
- Never allow your cash to remain idle.
- Good cash management can provide a major source of profit, while poor cash management can destroy a company in a matter of months.
- Be prepared to convert dollars into a stable foreign currency.
- Whenever possible, deal in cash payments.
- Anticipate competition between the buyer and seller over when payments will be made.
- Work continually to maintain positive real interest rates.
- Develop practices that enable you to internally finance working capital.
- Consider the possibility of acting as an acceptance company to facilitate your customers' purchases.
- Make the rapid collection of receivables a primary goal.
- Be aware that the stock market may become an uncertain source of capital.
- Develop relationships with several banks to facilitate capital availability in tightened capital markets.
- Make corresponding accounts and tax deposits a key negotiating point with your banks.

- Develop your ability to anticipate changes in monetary and fiscal policy and the effects on interest rates in financial markets.
- Be prepared to maintain more than one set of books.
- Inventory valuation should be based on NIFO rather than LIFO.
- Develop an appropriate inflationary adjustment for capital replacement or the value of your capital will disappear.

2

Marketing Strategies

*"The name of the game
in terms of planning during periods of high inflation is
guessing what ways the government is going
to try to correct their bad choices."*
— *Chief executive at Argentine bank*

Marketing under hyperinflation is a continuous balancing act, aimed at overcoming the ravaging effects of soaring inflation rates, while at the same time producing a product with a supportable price. Yesterday's profit-leader can become an instantaneous loser if all aspects of the marketing operation do not adequately compensate for rapidly increasing costs.

Pricing policies undergo a dramatic transformation during hyperinflation. Fluid pricing becomes an absolute necessity, and prices must change frequently and sharply to accurately reflect the impact of inflation. True costs become increasingly difficult to track, even as the need to do so grows more important.

The level of government regulation routinely increases as inflation rises, and anticipation of policy changes — as well as immediate reaction to them — becomes critical.

Hyperinflation creates a growing need for information of all kinds, not only the plans and policies of suppliers, competitors and the government, but even information regarding the current status of black markets, which often arise as a result of the market restrictions that tend to increase during hyperinflation.

The viability of various product lines is greatly affected when inflation rates take off, and those which sell slowly, have low profit margins, or have tightly controlled prices often disappear altogether.

Hyperinflation changes the time frame within which the marketing function must operate. Long-term becomes short-term, short-term becomes tomorrow, and the type of planning familiar to American business people becomes an effort in futility. In the ever-changing world of hyperinflation, prices, supplies, markets and government policies shift continually, presenting the corporate planner with a target that simply moves too quickly and unpredictably for accurate forecasting beyond a period of days, weeks, or, at most, months.

■ *Be prepared to execute prompt, selective price increases. It may even become necessary to do this on a daily or weekly basis.*

There is widespread agreement among South American executives that timely price changes are probably one of the most important methods for surviving high inflation. For them, however, effective pricing means weaving through a seemingly endless maze of regulations and restrictions. American business managers may one day be faced with similar complications in establishing their own pricing policies. Remember, the United States did have wage and price controls in 1971. (See Appendix.)

Throughout South America, prices often change before the ink in which they are recorded dries. At Bolivia's 50,000 percent inflationary peak, prices had to be adjusted hourly. (Exhibit 7 shows the incredible impact of hyperinflation on the cost of goods.) Customers commonly were quoted prices over the phone when ordering a part, understanding full well that by the time the part was picked up, the price would almost certainly be higher.

■ *Develop inflation-sensitive pricing policies.*

Pricing goods in a hyperinflationary environment is an extremely complex task. Some of the factors that companies must consider in structuring their prices are:

If the original price of merchandise was

$25

The price three months later would be

$118

Six months later

$560

One year later

$12,525

Exhibit 7: *At 50,000 percent inflation, the price on a necktie that cost $25 would rise to over $12,000 just one year later.*

- The appropriate costs to use as a base line for adjusting bills of materials to inflation.
- The future value of the currency.
- The cost of money.
- The best possible forecasts as to future costs of raw materials, parts, labor, utilities and transportation.
- The most reliable available indexes to forecast the industry and overall inflation rates.
- The opportunity costs of the capital used in the production process.
- Inflation adjustments for projects with long lead times.
- Monitoring of actions taken by competitors to reduce costs and therefore keep prices in check.

Should inflation begin to climb in the United States, it will be imperative that American companies adopt measures to factor these considerations into their pricing policies, so they are able to calculate prices that adequately reflect the true impact of inflation.

■ *It is necessary to establish a satisfactory current base price.*

The base price should not only reflect the current state of the economy but also expectations of inflation and unforeseen economic events other than inflation that could affect the real value of the price over time. Base prices should therefore include a contingency to account for these unforeseen events. Factors that should be considered when setting base prices include variance in rate of payment by different buyers, and changes in the costs of production that are not accurately reflected in the inflation index used to adjust prices.

■ *It is necessary to develop a basis for adjusting prices to account for inflation.*

When inflation is running high, all prices must be two-dimensional, reflecting the decreased value of money over time. This means that terms of sale for any payment other than cash paid at the time of sale must be scheduled or indexed to reflect inflation's impact. Not one single day can go by when an outstanding balance does not reflect inflation.

If it is necessary to issue a published price list, it will be imperative that the list be much more detailed than is currently the custom in the United States. Payment schedules may even have to include day-to-day increases, and in any case will have to be updated frequently to account for changes in inflation.

Rather than scheduling of prices, indexation is the norm in hyperinflationary economies, and a way of life in South America. In Brazil, in fact, it has been completely integrated into the economy. The universally accepted index there is a "monetary correction index" called OTN. Technically, the OTN is the interest rate on government bonds, which is fixed by the government on the first day of each month and is based on the inflation incurred during the past month. Prices are stated as "in OTNs," which means that the price is tied to the OTN index. The OTN reflects a combination of inflationary expectations and risk, and helps industry cope with the effects of inflation. Unfortunately, it also feeds inflation by transmitting past inflation rates to current rates of inflation.

In Brazil, a contract for payment "based on OTNs" means that, if a month lapses between the time a contract is signed and payment is received, the seller consults the OTN chart to see the percentage by which the price should increase to account for inflation. The payment price would then be raised by this percentage.

Individuals and companies even write checks "based on OTNs." This is the only way to guarantee that the check does not lose its value between the time it is written and the time it is cashed.

■ *If using an inflationary index, selecting and enforcing that index can be as important as establishing the base price.*

Indexes are by definition attempts to average the impact of inflation, and none are specific to any single company or contract. Each index reflects the change in prices of a particular basket of goods, which usually does not reflect the actual goods used by particular businesses. Because the prices of different materials accelerate at different rates, the actual impact of inflation on any company could be several times greater or less than the official index.

Under such circumstances, the profitability of any contract can depend as much on the index used as it does on the base price, and specialists exist to develop indexes for specific contracts. Use of an index that underestimates the seller's actual rate of inflation can easily turn a profitable deal into a loser.

South American companies have a variety of indexes to choose from. In Brazil, for example, there is the OTN; other indexes tied to the overall inflation rate, to the inflation rate of a particular raw material or group of products, or to the U.S. dollar exchange rate; and still others issued by the unions.

In spite of the variety of indexes, none is a perfect cure-all. Each index benefits certain companies — and certain contracts — more or less than others, so much so that companies are sometimes willing to give a 5 to 10 percent discount in exchange for being permitted to use the index they believe is most advantageous to a particular contract.

In the event of an inflationary upturn, American companies should be prepared to monitor their own specific inflation rates, to ensure that their contracts — if indexed — use an index that most accurately reflects those rates.

■ *Be prepared to react to wage and price controls.*

Wage and price controls are the almost universal reaction of governments facing runaway inflation. Italy, France and Britain all enacted controls in the years following World War II, and Brazil, Bolivia and Argentina have done so on a regular basis throughout the 1970s and '80s.

The United States instituted controls as recently as 1971, and American companies would be wise to anticipate their impact by reviewing the wage and price policies introduced by the federal government during that period. (See Appendix.)

South American companies have discovered that, during periods when they are subject to price controls, they fight a continuous battle with the government to have their prices adjusted as rapidly as possible to reflect the inflation that is taking place.

One strategy is to submit the highest supportable price in the hope it will be approved. One reason this is important is because South American governments tend to grant price increases based on the official inflation rate, which is often significantly below the actual cost increases the firm is experiencing.

'ARE WE STILL CATCHING UP WITH HIM OR IS HE CATCHING UP WITH US?'

Obtaining approval for a high price is also important because it becomes the base line for future price increases and for the discounts companies offer their favorite customers.

Once the price increase is approved by the government, the item is repriced and immediately submitted for another increase. This frequent changing of prices makes the use of a published price list very difficult, even for a short period of time. Prices are therefore more typically quoted by phone.

One Brazilian manufacturer indicated that during 1986 his company submitted two or three price increases. In 1987 it submitted one per month, and in 1988, due to spiraling inflation, submissions were up to two or three per month.

Under such circumstances, it becomes especially important that companies fully understand and document all of the elements of their own costs. This documentation is necessary evidence to substantiate requests for price increases, and without it, companies may have additional difficulty recouping their costs.

Preparing and filing requests becomes a constant way of life, since it often takes 30 to 40 days for approval. The procedure is so complicated and filled with so much bureaucratic wrangling that companies hire professional price consultants, who are actually lobbyists, to submit and argue the requests. These price consultants wield a great deal of power in this regulated environment.

■ *Large companies and multinationals should expect that their prices will be more closely regulated.*

The impact of price controls varies widely depending on company size, the type of product it produces, and whether it is a national or multinational firm. Larger companies tend to be subject to price controls, while many smaller companies operate virtually regulation-free. (This is not unlike the U.S. experience with wage and price controls in the early 1970s.) In Argentina, small firms tend to get their increases even when they are controlled, while large firms are often used to set examples.

Politics frequently play a role in the implementation of price increases. For example, in Brazil price increases on such consumer items as beer are very unpopular, so their implementation is often delayed until a period when demand falls off, such as just after Carnival.

Regardless of whether or not the government allows a particular price increase, the ability of a firm to charge higher prices is also a direct function of the amount of local and international competition it faces. Firms subject to stiff international competition are more limited in their ability to charge higher prices than those that are protected by trade laws.

■ *Be prepared for the possibility that competitors will sidestep price controls.*

Throughout Bolivia, Brazil and Argentina, circumvention of price controls is widespread. For example, until a recent regulatory change, many Argentine companies made slight modifications to or redesigned their products and then raised the prices, since new products were not governed by controls.

Another common way to circumvent controls is to turn new equipment into used. Because used equipment is not subject to controls in Brazil, one heavy machinery distributor routinely leases tractors to prospective buyers for a month or two, or uses them in his own yard, sometimes only to move dirt from one end of the yard to the other. He then sells the machines as used, often at twice the price he would be allowed to charge for new equipment.

■ *Be prepared for the appearance of black markets, and factor both official and black market exchange rates when establishing payment schedules.*

History has shown that market restrictions — a typical government reaction to inflation — almost inevitably lead to the creation of black markets, and Brazil, Bolivia and Argentina are no exceptions.

In the hyperinflationary economies of these South American countries, the black market rate often gives a more realistic basis for price adjustments than does the official rate. For this reason, monitoring the black market can become an important aspect of business management during periods of high inflation. Failure to consider black market rates when setting payment schedules can result in prices that fall far short of covering actual costs.

In 1985, when inflation was approaching 50,000 percent annualized, the black market rate in Bolivia changed as many as 50 times a day, yielding 50 price changes per day. Under such circumstances, failure to rapidly adjust prices could easily wipe out any profit margin.

The United States may never experience that order of economic instability, but if inflation rises, market restrictions and the subsequent appearance of black markets are likely results. Under those circumstances, businesses will have to monitor black market exchange rates in order to establish pricing structures that adequately protect profit margins.

■ *Dependable information on how competitors are adjusting their prices will become increasingly crucial.*

Though it is critical to adjust your own prices rapidly, if you do so more quickly than your competitors, you may lose market share. In high inflationary periods, when prices fluctuate rapidly, it becomes particularly difficult to track prices, yet failure to carefully monitor the prices of your competition can lead to costly pricing errors.

However, in certain cases where the competition's prices are insupportably low, it may be in a company's best interest to sacrifice some market share in order to maintain the proper cost/ price relationship.

■ Develop effective methods to keep track of the actual cost of production.

South American companies have had to use extensive analyses and sources of information to properly price their products. This is especially difficult to do under severe inflation because it is easy to lose track of changing costs. Proper pricing requires that a company monitor its own internal inflation to accurately determine its actual cost of production.

The difficulty of monitoring true costs is multiplied in high inflationary economies, because all prices do not move at a uniform rate. Averaging costs is therefore useless, because the component costs of some products may increase 100 percent during the same period in which others climb 1,000 percent.

■ Establish a base period from which to judge inflationary impact.

It is necessary to have a benchmark to use in measuring the inflationary impact on costs, prices and inventory valuation. This benchmark gives companies the ability to track their own internal rate of inflation, and provides them with data that can be used to justify price increases during periods when price controls are in effect.

To set a reliable benchmark, it would be best to establish this base around a period when inflation was relatively steady.

■ Prepare to monitor changes in the value of currency with increased vigilance.

During periods of high inflation there will be frequent and major changes in currency values. Shifting currency values can have a major impact on a company's ability to sell products in foreign markets, altering the relative price of those products in relation to competing products originating in other countries. American companies will need to develop a policy for reacting to these changes, either holding prices down to maintain market share or adjusting them upward to compensate for currency depreciation.

When currency values are unstable, it can also have a great effect on the prices of imported parts or components necessary for production. A flight out of the dollar — a likely result of climbing inflation rates — will have an especially harsh impact on those American businesses most reliant on imported parts.

■ Choose products with the largest profit margins.

Rapid changes in the inflation rate, compounded by government policies commonly instituted to fight inflation, can erase the margin on many products in a very short period of time.

In a hyperinflationary economy, the overall philosophy when determining which items should be produced and brought to the marketplace is that they should yield the largest gross profit. High-volume, low-margin items currently produced in the United States would most likely not be produced under hyperinflation. Because government-regulated price increases often do not cover cost increases, the risk of the margin disappearing overnight is just too great.

In Argentina and Brazil, many company presidents have established a minimum acceptable gross profit of 45 percent for any product. The size of the margin is necessary because interest costs on debt are extraordinarily high, and because companies must protect themselves from such factors as: future inflation; government-imposed price freezes that coincide with the skyrocketing of their own costs; rising supplier prices; and pressure imposed by customers to maintain current prices over time.

A fact of life in a hyperinflationary economy is the disappearance of products whose controlled price does not cover the cost of production. In Brazil, for example, dairy products such as milk, eggs and cheese became unavailable when the regulated price was set below their production cost.

Likewise, in the United States, high-volume products with extensive competition — characteristic of many consumer products — may be the first to disappear should inflation begin to rise, because they tend to have low profit margins.

■ *Be prepared to move from long-term contracts to short-term contracts.*

During high inflation, short-term contracts should be used whenever possible, and any intermediate or long-term contracts will have to be amended to include clauses allowing for inflationary adjustments.

Long-term contracts as they exist in the United States are rare in countries experiencing hyperinflation. In the few cases where long-term contracts are issued, specific language is included linking all costs to an index of some sort. Another alternative used in South America is to express the contract in U.S. dollars, a technique that obviously will not be helpful to American businesses.

No company sells on long-term fixed-price contracts in hyperinflationary economies. Any time a capital goods project has a long production horizon, a sizable down payment is required and an inflationary index is used to determine the value of the remaining balance. After a project is undertaken, the indexes are reviewed, negotiated and adjusted to reflect inflationary trends in the economy.

Should indexation become widespread in the United States, it is likely that new indexes will be developed because, among those that are currently most common, the consumer price index is unsuitable for manufacturers, and the GNP deflator's usefulness for specific industry price changes is limited.

■ *Sophisticated management information systems will be critical for responding to hyperinflation.*

Information is perhaps the most crucial ingredient in strategies for surviving hyperinflation, and it is especially important in the area of pricing. South American businesses often suffer because they are largely deficient in management information and are not widely computerized. Likewise, those American firms lacking sophisticated computerization will be at a major disadvantage, because in a rapidly changing world, those firms prepared to process and react to information the quickest fare the best.

At Bolivia's 1985 inflationary peak, one construction equipment firm had as many as 50 people in the field gathering up-to-date information on the current black market dollar-to-peso exchange rate. A central office was established, complete with a computer installation, and software was developed that could factor a variable price for hundreds of items.

The field people were in constant communication with those in the head office, advising them within minutes of any changes in the black market rate. On receipt of this information, the computer people adjusted their pricing data and new prices were established immediately.

If inflation does take off here, it will become necessary for American firms to develop or reprogram data management systems to analyze data and provide the up-to-the-minute information needed to respond to inflationary developments.

■ *Make planning a daily or weekly practice.*

In hyperinflationary economies, no company can afford the luxury of annual planning. The ability to forecast and perform forward planning becomes an effort in futility, because in one day's time, every variable in the forecast is capable of undergoing significant change.

Most companies operating in the hyperinflationary economies of South America consider a short-term forecast to be one week, and a long-term forecast three weeks.

According to an importer of plastic finished products in Bolivia, forecasting as little as one month in the future is impossible. "You'd be better off using your own crystal ball," he said.

A top executive of an Argentine multinational company says his superiors in the United States require a monthly forecast, but he knows it is obsolete the moment he puts it in the mail.

Planning becomes instead an almost daily activity. "The way we plan," says a top Brazilian businessman, "is to buy a newspaper in the morning, read the financial and political news, think about it while going to work, and then implement the plan as soon as we get to the office."

This is not to say the planning process is to be ignored, only that it is problematic.

Virtually every economic forecast in every country in the world is based on government projections. In Argentina, Brazil and Bolivia, though, government data and forecasts during times of hyperinflation have proven to be little more than guesswork. Often, the government changes the elements of its data, sometimes excluding an item from the basket of goods composing its inflation index if its price is extraordinarily high for a given month.

According to the president of a small Argentine company, the government's inflation forecasts are usually off by more than 50 percent, and indeed, the 1986 forecast of 28 percent ended up being far shy of the actual rate of 82 percent.

---

*"The economists are generally right
in their predictions but generally a good deal
out in their dates."*
— Sidney Webb, 1924

Under these conditions, most executives try to make their own best guesses as to future inflation rates, which is extremely difficult. During January 1988, for example, inflationary projections for the Brazilian economy ranged between 400 and 1,000 percent annually.

Should inflation begin to soar in the United States, American executives should be prepared to shorten the scope of their planning activities as well. Because of the instability and pace of change that prevail during inflationary periods, projections beyond a few weeks or months can easily prove meaningless, and the long-range planning policies now in widespread use will become virtually useless.

■ *Prepare to communicate verbally with all key operation managers on a daily basis.*

Because of the continuing, rapid pace of change in hyperinflationary economies, managers must be prepared to react instantly to both problems and opportunities. Knowledge and flexibility are critical, as well as the authority to act quickly without having to consult with superiors or deal with red tape. For these reasons, all members of management must be kept current on all phases of the company's business, policies and wishes, and must understand the breadth and nature of their responsibilities.

In most South American companies, for example, managers meet or communicate by phone to develop and discuss the company's plan on a daily basis.

Contrary to normal business practice in the United States, communication between managers in South America is almost always verbal. In the words of one South American executive, "you can't manage by sitting at your desk" during hyperinflation. Letters and memos between managers are virtually nonexistent, because the time involved in preparing, transmitting and reading them is simply too wasteful. It is important that American managers realize that, because of the rapidity of change brought on by high inflation, the window available for seizing an opportunity or solving a problem can easily close while written messages are exchanged.

■ *Seek appropriate amortization and depreciation techniques to accurately reflect inflationary effects on capital.*

One of the key difficulties South American companies have in pricing their products is their governments' refusal to allow them to factor in such items as amortization and depreciation of fixed assets at the inflated replacement costs.

The current United States depreciation policy — which is based on original purchase costs — will have to change to allow American companies to adjust their depreciation to accurately reflect the inflationary impact on their replacement costs.

Otherwise, the inability to recapture the true cost of capital can over time allow a company's capital stock to shrink to zero. Should this happen on a national basis, it will result in generally reduced investments in new equipment, thereby creating a recessionary environment throughout the United States.

SUMMARY

- Be prepared to execute prompt, selective price increases. It may even become necessary to do this on a daily or weekly basis.
- Develop inflation-sensitive pricing policies.
- It is necessary to establish a satisfactory current base price.
- It is necessary to develop a basis for adjusting prices to account for inflation.
- If using an inflationary index, selecting and enforcing that index can be as important as establishing the base price.
- Be prepared to react to wage and price controls.
- Large companies and multinationals should expect that their prices will be more closely regulated.
- Be prepared for the possibility that competitors will sidestep price controls.
- Be prepared for the appearance of black markets, and factor both official and black market exchange rates when establishing payment schedules.
- Dependable information on how competitors are adjusting their prices will become increasingly crucial.
- Develop effective methods to keep track of the actual cost of production.
- Establish a base period from which to judge inflationary impact.
- Prepare to monitor changes in the value of currency with increased vigilance.
- Choose products with the largest profit margins.
- Be prepared to move from long-term contracts to short-term contracts.
- Sophisticated management information systems will be critical for responding to hyperinflation.

- Make planning a daily or weekly practice.
- Prepare to communicate verbally with all key operation managers on a daily basis.
- Seek appropriate amortization and depreciation techniques to accurately reflect inflationary effects on capital.

© *News America Syndicate*

3

Manufacturing Decisions

*"In New York City you know the prices
and value, so you shop around. In Argentina you don't
care about the prices, just that you can buy."*
— *Argentine banking executive*

During periods of high inflation, manufacturing operations are particularly hard hit. In fact, in some extreme cases in South America, corporate attempts to survive have led some companies to shut down their manufacturing operations in favor of speculation, which can be a more profitable use of capital.

Purchasing efforts become increasingly difficult as inflation climbs, growing in importance at the same time. According to the South American experience, supplies and supply sources dwindle, government regulation increases, capital markets dry up, and costs change rapidly, often without notice.

High inflation tends to force changes in inventory policies and relations with foreign and domestic supply sources, making cost control efforts extremely difficult to manage. While conditions demand that the purchasing department be given greater authority and independence, they also increase opportunities for corruption.

■ *Anticipate that your purchasing department will assume a more dominant role in the long-run survival of your firm.*

Materials constitute the single largest portion of total costs and, because the supply and cost of materials can fluctuate so wildly during hyperinflation, effective purchasing practices become absolutely critical to business survival. An inefficient purchasing department can easily lead a company into bankruptcy.

In the United States, there are typically many sources of supply for any particular item. As far as a purchasing department is concerned, competition is the name of the game. Efficient, creative purchasers can save a company substantial amounts of money through the proper sourcing of material.

In South America, however, a purchasing department often finds itself in a situation with only one or two suppliers, thereby limiting the degree of price competitiveness.

There is a good possibility that similar circumstances will prevail in the United States should wage and price controls be instituted — as they were in 1971 — because shortages are the natural result of such controls.

In some South American markets, the situation has grown even worse. Because there is a limited number of suppliers, there is a tendency for some of them to form associations that operate as cartels. These cartels establish a market price, and often a company's only choice is to pay that price or shut down.

In Brazil, these supplier associations exercise additional market power by prohibiting their customers from producing parts that could be supplied by any member of the association.

Though cartels are illegal in the United States, it is safe to assume that, in the event of anti-inflationary regulations, shortages and other supply problems will develop here, making the purchasing function much more difficult to carry out, and the department's performance even more critical to any business's success.

■ Purchasing agents should be prepared to deal with price controls.

As mentioned earlier, price controls are a natural government reaction to inflation. Though this does not guarantee that price controls will be instituted in the United States, purchasing departments would be best off to anticipate controls and thereby avoid being blindsided should they be introduced. (See the Appendix for a description of the 1971 U.S. wage and price regulations.)

Perhaps the greatest impact of price controls upon the purchasing function is that they result in shortages and change the expectations of suppliers. The situation is exacerbated by the frequent desire of both customers and suppliers to use inventory as an inflation hedge. While buyers want to obtain inventory before price increases are granted, suppliers often attempt to hold inventory until they are able to raise prices.

Some South American manufacturers purchase raw materials ahead of time based on the anticipation of receiving an order. Though this is not the normal purchasing practice in the United States, it can be crucial in a hyperinflationary economy, where a company cannot depend on having its purchase orders filled at a moment's notice. Purchasing managers in South America always try to keep one step ahead of suppliers, because suppliers who have information about upcoming government-approved price increases will often delay accepting orders.

During periods of wage and price controls, companies have to engage in anticipating governmental action. When controls are in effect, if a company's information suggests that a controlled price will be increased shortly, purchasing activity should be increased immediately.

In Brazil, for example, one producer of machine parts found out that the government was about to grant a 60 percent increase on stainless steel, and instantly placed an order for $300,000 worth — though he had no immediate use for the steel — in an effort to avoid the $180,000 increase.

■ *Be prepared to examine foreign supply sources and shift the balance of your purchases toward domestic suppliers.*

Another by-product of hyperinflation that complicates purchasing activities is the decreased availability and affordability of imported goods. Hyperinflation is often characterized by changes in exchange rates and protectionist regulations that make foreign supplies both expensive and hard to get, so those businesses that depend most heavily on imports can expect to be particularly hard-hit by high inflation.

In Argentina and Brazil, foreign suppliers are at a particular disadvantage because the government subjects them to tight

51

quotas and high taxes. Argentine firms are reluctant to buy from U.S. suppliers, for example, because the government imposes a 180-day delay in payment in order to improve, at least in the short term, the country's international balance of payments. The risk the company faces from this delay is that a currency devaluation could greatly increase the dollar cost of the imported goods.

Should inflation begin to rise in the United States, American companies with a major reliance on foreign suppliers should anticipate especially high prices and increased difficulties obtaining imported supplies, and whenever possible should develop domestic alternatives as a contingency.

■ *The director of purchasing should be given the authority to move quickly and independently to take advantage of opportunities.*

During hyperinflation, events occur so rapidly that a company's executives must be given the responsibility and authority to act quickly and decisively. In particular, inventory decisions must be made promptly, or immense additional costs may be incurred. Under these circumstances, there is often no time for the red tape and chain-of-command approvals common in the United States.

ROTHCO
ORIGINAL

"I DON'T WANT TO INTERRUPT, MYRTLE, BUT SHOULDN'T WE GET ON WITH OUR SHOPPING BEFORE THE PRICES GO UP AGAIN?"

For example, in January 1987, the general manager of a Brazilian equipment firm learned of an impending price increase. He instantly picked up the phone and placed an order for a large quantity of raw material for immediate delivery. This practice in the United States might entail filing a request to corporate superiors, which would probably take weeks for approval. In a hyperinflationary economy, however, the opportunity would have disappeared long before such approval was granted, since the new prices would have already gone into effect, costing the firm what could have been a substantial savings.

South American businesses cannot afford to delay decision-making, and for that reason there is much less red tape and more delegation of responsibility and authority than is common in the United States. Capable, assertive managers are crucial in this type of inflationary environment.

Though current purchasing policies in the U.S. do not require such immediacy, if the nation's inflation increases significantly, American companies should be prepared to shorten channels of approval so purchasing decisions can be made rapidly.

■ *Allow the director of purchasing to commit to suppliers with verbal purchase orders.*

Verbal purchase orders are typical in a hyperinflationary environment, because the time consumed to prepare even a minimal amount of paperwork can be extremely costly. However, verbal purchase orders are only practical when the company or division president has complete confidence in his purchasing manager and has given him or her a high degree of responsibility and authority.

In Argentina, companies have another reason for using verbal, rather than written, communications. The government imposes a 1 percent tax on the face value of any written purchase order. Verbal purchase orders and internal records are often used to offset the formal process and avoid paying the tax.

■ *Be aware that hyperinflation creates increased opportunities for corruption.*

Because of the fluctuation in costs and the rapid pace of change, it is very difficult to adequately monitor cash transactions when inflation is high. Increased vigilance, audits and crosschecks must be capable of picking up undue variance in prices that may point to employee corruption.

Unfortunately, in all countries, because the bulk of the sales dollar revolves around the purchasing department, and because buyers need freedom to negotiate if they are expected to reduce costs, the purchasing area is particularly susceptible to corruption. This is especially true if purchasing departments are given wide leeway as to when and with whom they place large orders. For this reason, in many privately held South American companies, someone from the owner's family is placed on the purchasing department staff in order to prevent corruption.

Whether a family member or not, it is vital that every person in a company's purchasing department be beyond reproach. This is particularly important in hyperinflationary economies, where the maze of regulations and rapidly fluctuating prices creates a situation in which dishonesty can easily go undetected.

■ *Change inventory policies if necessary to permit the accumulation of large inventories during times of hyperinflation.*

In high inflationary economies, inventory becomes not only a source for production, but also a speculative device, because its value frequently increases faster than the value of other investments.

Depending on current prices, cash is often used to purchase large amounts of inventory, usually in the form of raw materials. A standard manufacturing tenet in the United States is that inventory should be kept as low as possible. But in a hyperinflationary economy, there are two strong incentives for stockpiling inventory. It can protect profit margins that might otherwise be eroded by sudden price increases from suppliers, and it can protect the company from shortages, which often arise when wage and price controls are used to combat inflation.

In South America, when price controls are not in effect, it is normal practice to convert cash to inventory as quickly as possible. (When controls are in effect, inventory does not gain value as rapidly, and therefore loses some of its speculative value.)

In fact, when the inflation rate is greater than the interest rate — negative interest — it is common for companies to borrow money in order to purchase inventory and/or merchandise. This is an important way to maximize future profits. A company would gladly borrow money at 18 percent monthly interest if that inventory was going to soon experience a 60 percent price increase.

Another reason for keeping large inventories is to ensure a steady production schedule. Under hyperinflation, suppliers also use inventory as a speculative device, and, during periods when prices are controlled, often sit on their inventory in anticipation of the government approving a new price increase.

While the stockpiling of inventory can be instrumental to a company's survival, it is by no means always appropriate. In trying to decide whether to increase or decrease inventory, a company has to consider both the earning potential of that inventory relative to other investments, and the necessity of having inventory available to maintain a steady production flow.

■ Effective cost control requires that you develop methods for estimating your internal rate of inflation.

One of the primary goals of every company in every country is to reduce costs. Smart managers recognize that cost reduction is the most effective way to positively affect a company's bottom line. A dollar saved through cost reduction is literally a dollar earned, while a comparable dollar increase in sales volume may or may not translate into additional profits. It certainly will not increase profits by one dollar, since additional sales volume will mean corresponding increases in a variety of costs.

In the United States, a number of techniques are used to reduce and control manufacturing costs. The objective is to produce a product for the lowest possible cost, enabling a company to realize the greatest profit and/or to reduce its price and maintain or increase market share.

During hyperinflation, however, it is difficult to track the true costs of production, and consequently price increases tend to be substituted for cost-reduction efforts, which can lead to less efficient production techniques.

(For more information on cost reduction, see *The Harry Figgie Guide to Cost Reduction and Profit Improvement.*)

In order to effectively monitor true costs during a hyper-inflationary period, it is necessary for companies to develop methods of estimating their own internal inflation rates. One large Brazilian manufacturer developed an index to track its internal rate, and found that, in 1987, the company's own inflation was 525 percent, while the country's official rate was 365 percent. In other words, it was forced to sell its product at a loss for several months until its next round of price increases was approved. Had the company failed to monitor its own inflation rate, it would not have known it was operating at a loss, and would not have had the evidence necessary to gain government approval for the price increase that covered its true production costs.

American companies will generally have an advantage over their South American counterparts in tracking their internal inflation rates, because the former have more fully integrated computerized data analysis into everyday management. This is another reason that companies in the United States should make sure their computer capabilities are up to date. At most companies in Argentina, Bolivia and Brazil, cost-reduction techniques are in limited use. Work sampling, organizational and ratio analyses, and other inexpensive yet effective cost-reduction measures, so critical to U.S. operations, are in the infant stages. A large part of this failure to stress cost reduction is related to the wide price fluctuations found in hyperinflationary economies. One can imagine the frustrations of a president intent on cost control but facing almost daily increases in his labor, material and burden costs.

ROTHCO
ORIGINAL
"I'M AFRAID I MAY HAVE TO LET SOME OF YOU GO!"

Other impediments to cost control are the strong unions and heavy government regulation typically found in South America. In all three countries studied, it remains very difficult and expensive to lay off employees, making it especially hard to reduce labor costs. Similar circumstances may develop in the United States, because it is not unlikely that both union strength and government regulation will increase here should inflation rise significantly.

**■ *Large corporations and multinationals should expect to
have greater need for cost reduction.***

The fact that it is difficult to control costs during hyperinflation
is self-evident. This does not mean, however, that cost reduction
should be ignored. In the vast majority of small South American
companies, cost reduction is not emphasized, but at large
corporations — especially multinationals — ignoring cost reduction
can be suicidal.

Under wage and price controls, multinationals and larger
companies are frequently used to set an example. Their requests
for price increases are more likely to be constrained than those of
local companies. Small local suppliers are frequently permitted to
raise prices without being subject to normal government review.
This creates a problem for large companies, since they often incur
cost increases which they cannot pass on in the form of price
increases of their own.

Extra scrutiny of these companies was common in all three
South American countries, as well as in the United States during
the 1971 wage and price controls. Cost-reduction measures may
therefore be the only way large companies can maintain profit
margins when government price controls are in effect.

Also, it is often only the large multinationals that have the
ability to implement sophisticated control measures and
computerized systems, which can be a tremendous asset in
identifying cost-reduction opportunities. For example, a top
executive of one large multinational stationed in Sao Paulo, Brazil
— unable to afford new equipment — developed a computerized
control system that enabled the company to more economically
utilize existing machinery, resulting in greatly improved operating
results.

**■ *Though cost reduction remains a key to improving profits,
companies must always be prepared for opportunities to
raise prices.***

Regardless of its importance, cost reduction can in no way offset
the effects of inflation on a company's profit margin during
hyperinflation. A firm must be prepared to react almost
instantaneously any time there is an opportunity to increase
prices.

In Brazil, for example, at the end of 1987 the government suddenly lifted price controls, presenting companies with a long-awaited opportunity to raise their prices. Forty-five days later controls were once again imposed. Those companies that failed to take advantage of this window of opportunity lost out on a chance to recoup their own higher costs. One lost opportunity can easily put a company out of business.

Ironically, when price controls are introduced, inefficient firms can in some cases actually benefit. The inefficient firm has more opportunity to reduce costs, since the operation has so much fat that can be eliminated easily. In fact, price controls can be a catalyst toward reducing costs in all companies, since that may be the only way to maintain profits.

■ Anticipate difficulty in maintaining capital expenditure programs.

As inflation rises, access to funds shrinks and long-term investment projects become harder to finance. Though the extent of capital expenditures differs widely in Argentina, Bolivia and Brazil, the instability caused by hyperinflation has resulted in a serious flight of resources from all three countries. This problem has been particularly severe in Argentina and Bolivia because of the relatively easy access to dollars as an alternative form of investment.

In Argentina, Bolivia and Brazil, local banks are a limited source of investment capital. Reserve requirements are extremely high — 75 percent in Argentina, for example, compared to 12 percent in the United States. Furthermore, a bank's available funds are usually lent to the government to support its fiscal budget.

While South American companies might occasionally borrow in local currency for short-term investments, they have to borrow in U.S. dollars from an international source when looking for a long-term or sizable loan. Multinational corporations, of course, have the possibility of obtaining needed capital from their parent company.

American companies should expect domestic banks to play a decreasing role in the financing of long-term projects. There is already a trend among American companies to rely increasingly on foreign capital, and this trend can be expected to accelerate in the face of any inflation-triggered flight of capital from the United

States. However, foreign investors are likely to be more hesitant to invest in American companies as inflationary instability increases. The probable result will be a credit squeeze, with long-term funding especially difficult to obtain.

■ *Be aware that speculation in commodities and currencies may provide a better rate of return than capital projects.*

American firms may also need to alter their thinking regarding capital expenditures because, in severe inflation, the rate of return from capital projects may fall far short of the rate of return on speculation in commodities and other currencies. Under such conditions, capital development is often sacrificed because profitability and even survival may depend on speculation.

SUMMARY

- Anticipate that your purchasing department will assume a more dominant role in the long-run survival of your firm.
- Purchasing agents should be prepared to deal with price controls.
- Be prepared to examine foreign supply sources and shift the balance of your purchases toward domestic suppliers.
- The director of purchasing should be given the authority to move quickly and independently to take advantage of opportunities.
- Allow the director of purchasing to commit to suppliers with verbal purchase orders.
- Be aware that hyperinflation creates increased opportunities for corruption.
- Change inventory policies if necessary to permit the accumulation of large inventories during times of hyperinflation.
- Effective cost control requires that you develop methods for estimating your internal rate of inflation.
- Large corporations and multinationals should expect to have greater need for cost reduction.

- Though cost reduction remains a key to improving profits, companies must always be prepared for opportunities to raise prices.

- Anticipate difficulty in maintaining capital expenditure programs.

- Be aware that speculation in commodities and currencies may provide a better rate of return than capital projects.

4

Industrial Relations

*"Inflation is an immoral tax
that leads to immoral values."*
— *South American bank officer*

Like most other areas of business management, industrial relations are greatly affected by hyperinflation. The characteristic inflationary spiral exerts continuous pressure upon businesses to keep wages in line with prices. Regardless of what steps are taken, the wage/price gap never quite closes.

The result is often increased tension between management and labor, and a general deterioration in employee morale.

The impact of hyperinflation on wages and benefits is immense. For example, Brazilian employees who were not given raises in the first three months of 1988 watched their buying power plummet 64 percent. Even worse was the spring of 1985, when Bolivians saw their real income drop 90 percent in only three months.

Perhaps even more ominous is the fact that, throughout South America, the assets of pension funds — as well as savings accounts and insurance policies — have dropped in value to near worthlessness.

The pace of labor/management negotiations is both faster and more frantic under hyperinflationary conditions. The demands upon management to grant wage increases are virtually continuous, yet government regulations tie employers' hands, often controlling their ability both to grant raises and to pass higher labor costs on via price increases.

ROTHCO

In South America, the demand for wage increases is typically initiated by government unions and, when granted, private industry is forced to follow suit. Whether it is the government or a particular industry or business that initiates the action, increases give way to higher prices, which in turn create inflationary expectations and pave the way for further wage increase demands. This continuous wage/price spiral, if unchecked, can build ever-increasing government deficits, and increases the cost of doing business, eroding private sector profits as well.

■ *Labor relations staffs should be prepared to face stronger unions and virtually continuous negotiations.*

In hyperinflationary economies, individuals tend to seek the support of a group to represent them in order to survive constantly rising prices.

This is certainly true in Bolivia, Brazil and Argentina, where the union movement is very strong in both the public and private sectors. Some South American business leaders go so far as to complain that union leaders actually use hyperinflation to their own advantage, recognizing it as a major source of their power.

Because wages continually lag behind rising prices during hyperinflation, there is a near-constant need for negotiations, as union members press their leaders to push for higher wages.

Like South America's, unions in the United States have historically grown more dominant during unstable economic times. It is therefore reasonable to expect that the instability and uncertainty that would likely result from high rates of inflation in America would once again lead to increased union activity.

■ There is a high likelihood that wages will at some point be frozen, and labor will apply pressure on management to circumvent controls.

Wage freezes are as common as price controls among governments struggling to control inflation, so it is reasonable to anticipate the enactment of freezes in the United States. As mentioned earlier, President Nixon imposed wage controls in 1971 with inflation at only 4.7 percent.

The pressure on companies to circumvent these controls tends to be intense, and sidestepping regulations has become all but routine in South America. Companies in Bolivia, Brazil and Argentina have devised a number of paths around wage controls, including: pay bonuses for such things as punctual attendance; changing job classifications; pay for hours not actually worked; interest-free loans; and loans that are not expected to be repaid.

These tactics are widespread for two reasons: Price controls do not stop inflation, which causes the real wages of workers to decline; and once one firm breaks the wage control guidelines, other companies are forced to follow suit in order to keep good employees.

Under wage and price controls, a company is in the untenable position of having to negotiate with the unions for wage increases and with the government for price increases. Often it is caught in the middle. During one adjustment period in 1987, the Argentine government allowed a 4 percent wage increase. The unions were demanding 10 percent, but the government made it clear to businesses that anything more than 4 percent could not be passed on in the form of price increases, and therefore would have to come from company profits.

A similar situation existed in the United States during the 1971 controls, which dictated a general guideline of 5.5 percent annual wage increases, but only 2.5 percent annual price increases. Individual companies were expected to make up for the 3 percent difference either from their profits or through gains in their productivity.

■ *Larger companies should anticipate being used to set an example, as happened in 1971.*

As pointed out earlier, small companies tend not to be subject to wage and price controls, and therefore are able to pay their workers more than large firms. The former also tend to have more flexibility to increase their prices so they accurately reflect the higher costs.

Larger companies, on the other hand, are often used as examples, and are routinely subject to stricter controls. Not only is this true in Brazil, Argentina and Bolivia, but it was also true when wage and price controls were enacted in the United States in 1971.

Larger companies, especially multinationals, should be prepared to face especially stringent controls in the event such regulations are introduced.

■ *Prepare to shorten pay periods.*

During hyperinflation, the purchasing power of wages tends to deteriorate rapidly. Workers are driven to spend their pay immediately, before it loses its value, and before prices climb beyond their reach. Given the lag between wage adjustments and price increases, employers are pressured to shorten pay periods.

During the worst of Bolivia's hyperinflationary crisis, for example, workers were paid every two or three days. Though events in the United States may never require such drastic adjustments, American firms should be aware that shortened pay periods are commonly a result of rising inflation rates.

■ *Anticipate morale problems among middle management, which often bears the greatest burden during hyperinflation.*

Because they have limited negotiating power of their own, and no union representation to pursue their demands for higher wages, middle management often suffers the greatest relative losses when inflation takes off. Companies that wish to retain and foster that management level should be careful to maintain equitable wage policies.

■ *Consider the type of index you will use for cost-of-living adjustments, and be prepared to make adjustments often.*

Should inflation take off in the United States, it is likely that the type of index used to make cost-of-living adjustments — and the frequency with which they are made — will become issues that American businesses will have to settle.

South Americans use a wide variety of indexes for their cost-of-living adjustments. In Brazil, for example, the OTN is the official index, but there are several others — some created by the unions — that are used to adjust wages on an individual basis.

No matter which index is used, the adjustments are made often, with a wide variation in frequency, depending on the rate of inflation, the type of industry, and the nature of government wage and price controls. During the worst of Bolivia's hyperinflationary crisis, most workers received wage increases three times per month. In Argentina, some employees receive increases only once per quarter, and in Brazil, wage increases are triggered when the government's inflation index increases by 20 percent.

Regardless of the frequency of wage hikes, they rarely keep pace with inflation. For example, if an increase is given every three months while inflation is running at 18 percent monthly — as it frequently is in South America — employee purchasing power will drop by 39 percent compounded between wage hikes. Even if workers then receive a 39 percent raise, they lost a great deal in terms of real wages during those three months, and their adjusted wage will begin to lose its value immediately after it is granted.

As a result, even when receiving the maximum inflation adjustment, a worker's salary does not keep pace with inflation. When salary increases are less than the inflation rate, the situation is even worse.

This lag between income hikes and the inflation rate has been used by managers as a bizarre sort of personnel tool. One Argentine banker hired a new employee at 10,000 australes per month (then worth about $2,700) but soon realized he had made a mistake. "All I had to do was wait two months without increasing his salary. Now, even though he's not working out, at least I'm not paying him very much. Presto, I made a good decision."

■ Anticipate the effects of money illusions among your employees.

One of the problems in controlling wage demands in a high inflationary economy is that workers suffer from a money illusion. When they receive inflated wage increases — especially during the early phases of hyperinflation — they tend to believe that their real income is increasing, even though it is generally being eroded.

The opposite side of the money illusion occurs once inflation rates begin to fall and wage increases begin to slow or shrink. Though their purchasing power may actually be rising, employees often become disgruntled because they are accustomed to larger increases.

This is particularly true for hourly workers. More sophisticated workers tend to translate their wages from the local currency into U.S. dollars in order to determine for themselves whether in real terms they were paid more this pay period than last.

The money illusion is a common condition during inflation in all economies, and its chief impact is that, when the inflation rate begins to subside, companies are still pressured to maintain the pace of wage increases that was necessary during the height of inflation.

■ *Fringe benefits must be adjusted to reflect inflation or they can disappear.*

In hyperinflationary economies, it is difficult to determine the value of any particular wage, and almost impossible to keep it in step with inflation. For this reason, fringe benefits become an even more important element of the compensation package. Like wages, though, if they are not indexed somehow to counteract inflation, they can rapidly lose their value.

The most serious fringe benefit problem during hyperinflation is taking care of workers after they reach retirement age. The hyperinflation that has occurred in Argentina, Bolivia and Brazil has wiped out the assets of hundreds, if not thousands, of pension funds, to say nothing of individual savings accounts. In Bolivia, prior to the 1983 de-dollarization of the peso, retirement plans were often held in dollars. When the de-dollarization plan transferred all dollar-denominated accounts into peso accounts, at one-tenth the black market exchange rate, pensions became virtually worthless.

Because of this erosion of pensions, in all three countries adequate means for retirement do not exist for the vast majority of people. Only a handful of companies have any kind of pension program, and government plans are woefully inadequate, if not totally bankrupt. Consequently, employees either have to initiate and fund their own form of retirement plan or, more typically, have large families to support them in their old age, or keep working until death.

In the United States, consideration will have to be given to indexation of pension funds to compensate for the effects of inflation. It will also be necessary that the rate of return on the pension fund assets match the index, or those assets will be drained and perhaps depleted.

SUMMARY

- Labor relations staffs should be prepared to face stronger unions and virtually continuous negotiations.
- There is a high likelihood that wages will at some point be frozen, and labor will apply pressure on management to circumvent controls.
- Larger companies should anticipate being used to set an example, as happened in 1971.
- Prepare to shorten pay periods.
- Anticipate morale problems among middle management, which often bears the greatest burden during hyperinflation.
- Consider the type of index you will use for cost-of-living adjustments, and be prepared to make adjustments often.
- Anticipate the effects of money illusions among your employees.
- Fringe benefits must be adjusted to reflect inflation or they can disappear.

Conclusion

Though this report frequently refers to "hyperinflation," the United States is unlikely to suffer hyperinflation as it is classically defined, or even as it has occurred over the past decade in South America, with inflation rates consistently running toward 1,000 percent and beyond.

As business and financial leaders throughout Bolivia, Brazil and Argentina pointed out, though, it will not take triple-digit inflation to wreak havoc on the United States economy. A sudden acceleration into the teens and twenties would be sufficient to alter personal and corporate lifestyles, and would necessitate changes in the way Americans run their businesses and their lives.

An inflationary surge of this scope is easily possible given current U.S. economic conditions. Indeed, many South American leaders are convinced that rising inflation rates are the logical by-product of what they see as our ruinous fiscal policies. Again and again, these business and financial leaders expressed dismay that America's headlong sprint down the classic inflationary path was receiving so little attention in the United States, while it seemed so obvious from their vantage point at the end of that road.

If there is one overriding lesson from South America, it is that governments cannot indefinitely continue to spend beyond their means without suffering terrible economic consequences. There is simply no logical reason to think that the United States can become the first country in world history to successfully manage its economy by continuing to rely on the resources of other nations to finance its excesses.

*"Any government, like any family,
can for a year spend a little more than it earns. But you
and I know that a continuance of that habit
means the poorhouse."*
— *Franklin D. Roosevelt, 1932*

The impact of hyperinflation on every aspect of a nation's life is immense. As far as the business arena, hyperinflation makes a mockery of traditionally sound business practices, and makes day-to-day decision-making an impossible choice between short-term survival and long-term suicide.

At the most basic level, the development of rising inflation rates would alter the fundamental climate in which U.S. businesses operate. In all likelihood, the level of government involvement would increase significantly, introducing a maze of regulations and wage and price controls that severely restricts management's discretionary powers. The force of the nation's unions would probably increase as well, as a steady erosion of real wages drives workers to forge a united front.

Many once-profitable businesses and product lines will become losers and will be abandoned. Products without substantial profit margins will disappear from the shelves, and production will be increasingly ignored in favor of speculation, as the latter comes to play a greater role in corporate profit-making.

At the same time, prices will skyrocket, putting many goods and services out of reach, even as supplies tighten and in some cases dry up altogether.

Interest rates will enter an upward spiral, resulting in a shortage of affordable credit. New business starts will plummet and unemployment will surge.

The complexion of entire industries will change. Banks, for instance, may find themselves facing competition from corporations anxious to make loans, as interest rates exceed the returns available through normal business operation. Stockbrokers will find themselves out of work, as the instability of the market drives investors into the many high-interest investments available in a credit-tightened economy. Venture capitalists will also be forced into new businesses by the unavailability of capital and the low level of new business starts and capital investments. By the same token, entrepreneurs will find themselves unable to obtain the funding needed to fuel their activities.

Manufacturers will suffer increasing hardships. Prices will shoot through the roof, and supplies and supply sources will dwindle and in some cases disappear. The returns on manufacturing goods are likely to be far outpaced by the returns on speculation, so cash and manpower will be diverted to investment activities.

Companies that rely on imported parts will find those parts unavailable or exceedingly expensive, because of the dollar's decreased international buying power, and the restrictive import legislation that is likely to be introduced. The latter will also have a major impact on importers of goods and services.

Retailers will find themselves faced with ever-increasing costs, shortages, discontinued product lines, and a lack of credit to finance both their own inventory purchases and the purchases of their customers. To survive, they will be forced to limit the variety of products they sell, and to substantially and continually raise their prices.

The construction market will be particularly hard-hit, as costs are driven to unimaginable levels and credit to fund supply needs grows insupportably expensive or unavailable. At the same time, interest rates will climb so high, and loanable funds become so scarce, that few individuals or businesses are able to purchase a new home or building. Those that have the necessary capital are likely to find that, in a credit drought, the alternative earning potential of their own cash is simply too valuable to be wasted on construction.

The same environment that drives companies to change the focus of their operations will force many employees and managers to abandon company loyalty for the sake of survival. Income, benefits and cost-of-living policies will become increasingly important, and workers will be more likely to change jobs for a more favorable compensation and benefit package than they are in today's relatively stable climate. Wage and price controls — which often result in companies being unable to pass on demanded pay hikes through increased prices — may further complicate the picture.

High inflation rates also tend to have a weakening effect on both employee and corporate morality. Though this is not to suggest that inflation will cause an explosion in crime, there is a marked tendency during inflationary periods for both individuals and companies to engage in activity that borders on illegal — bending rules and sidestepping regulations, for example. Black markets are commonplace in inflationary societies, and it is not unlikely that the advent of high inflation in the U.S. would be accompanied by an increase in immoral or illegal behavior, as companies and individuals struggle to maintain their standard of living.

While hyperinflation turns business management into a struggle with chaos, there are certain basic measures that can enable most companies to survive. Under such circumstances, the key to survival is flexibility. Top management must develop a willingness to throw away the rule book whenever necessary, adopting in its place a fluid, elastic management style.

Managers on all levels must be given the latitude to make and act upon decisions quickly. During the chaos and rapid change brought on by high inflation, executives cannot manage from their desks. Those who are prone to letter and memo writing, who are unable to take action on short notice, or who require approval from their superiors will be the most likely to fail under high inflationary conditions.

Likewise, companies that have strict approval, communications and reporting requirements will find themselves at a disadvantage, because of the need for management to react quickly to both problems and opportunities. In general, centralized power of authority will have a detrimental effect on a company's ability to survive and succeed during hyperinflation. Decision-making authority cannot simply emanate from the top, but must be distributed throughout the organization so as to avoid time-consuming bottlenecks. Likewise, there is no time for ponderous red tape requirements.

Managers on all levels should be carefully instructed as to corporate objectives and guidelines, and then allowed to carry out their functions independently, with a full understanding of the corporation's wishes. It is also critically important that every manager — indeed, every employee — understands the impact of inflation, especially the time value of money.

Though hyperinflation presents perilous stumbling blocks, there are also opportunities for substantial profits. The key to survival and profitability is cash management. Cash must earn interest at every moment, which most often means it is invested in a foreign nation with a more stable economy, or in hard goods that are in constant demand. Wherever it is invested, cash must be moved around frequently as windows of opportunity open and close.

Again, the hedge most frequently used in South America — investment in dollars — will be unavailable to U.S. businesses and individuals, making inflation an even more complex problem for Americans.

The management strategy that is most likely to succeed during hyperinflation will include some of the following characteristics:

■ *Cash management will be perhaps <u>the</u> focus of business operation.*

- Never allow your cash to stay idle.
- Keep receivables at a minimum.
- Be aware that speculation may provide a better rate of return than production or capital projects.
- Be prepared to operate with little or no credit, and anticipate difficulty financing capital expenditures.

■ *Management responsibility must be widely delegated.*

- Spread decision-making authority throughout the layers of management.
- Educate all managers as to corporate objectives and guidelines.
- Make absolutely certain your managers understand the time value of money.

■ *Fluid pricing will become critical.*

- Be prepared to execute prompt, selective price increases.
- Establish systems to monitor true costs and competitors' prices.
- Sales must be in cash, or must be billed according to an index or schedule that accounts for inflationary devaluation.

■ *Expect operations to be affected by supply irregularities and shortages.*

- Be prepared to accumulate large amounts of inventory.
- Anticipate the interruption or discontinuation of operations.
- Be prepared for black markets.

■ *Make planning a constant way of life.*

- Planning should be done daily or weekly.
- Long-term planning should cover a period of months, while short-term should cover a period of weeks.

■ *Monitor and anticipate government action.*

- Be prepared for wage and price controls.
- Choose products with large profit margins, to guard against prohibitive price controls.
- Move away from imported goods, which may be subject to quotas or high tariffs.

Sadly, though, all these specific steps, while vitally necessary, are only survival techniques, and do nothing to address the fundamental problems of an economy gone haywire. That is the job of the government. Until the government takes the responsibility of addressing the nation's monumental debt, however, individuals and corporations are left to cope as best they can — or simply to survive — and to alert their leaders to this growing crisis.

This first report was designed to provide corporate executives with some insights into managing a corporation under high inflation, based on the experiences of the business and financial leadership of three nations that have struggled long and hard with some of the most ruinous inflation rates in history.

Our next step will be to delve more deeply into the underlying causes of hyperinflation, its political costs and its implications for individuals. Our ultimate goal is to educate the U.S. public and policymakers as to the devastating inflationary consequences of prolonged deficit spending, and to come to some conclusions as to how runaway inflation can be prevented from occurring in the United States.

If this manual helps sound the alarm, and offers some insights into how hyperinflation can be survived, then it will have fulfilled its purpose.

Appendix

Governments typically react to runaway inflation with legislative bandages, the most common of which are wage and price controls. Brazil, Argentina and Bolivia have instituted controls repeatedly over the past decade, and similar regulations have been used by several European nations throughout the 1900s. The United States has likewise resorted to wage and price controls on several occasions, most recently in 1971.

Should inflation accelerate in the U.S., it would be wise to prepare for the possible introduction of controls by becoming familiar with the 1971 restrictions.

1971 U.S. WAGE AND PRICE CONTROLS

On August 15, 1971, President Richard M. Nixon shocked the nation and the world with this announcement: "The time has come for decisive action — action that will break the vicious circle of spiraling wages and costs. I am today ordering a freeze on all prices and wages throughout the United States for a period of 90 days."

The freeze, accompanied by a series of regulations, was implemented to combat the nation's 4.7 percent inflation and 5.8 percent unemployment rates, to stimulate the economy and to improve the nation's international balance of payments.

The President's move was "one of the most radical reversals of policy in all political history," according to *Business Week,* which predicted the measures would "produce radical changes in the climate in which business operates."

The key points of the President's economic intervention included:

- An immediate 90-day freeze on wages, prices, salaries and rents.
- A 10 percent surcharge on most dutiable imports.
- A 10 percent investment tax credit on new American-built capital equipment.
- Repeal of the 7 percent excise tax on automobiles (which would reduce domestic car prices by about $200 per car).
- A $4.7 billion cut in federal spending, featuring a 5 percent cut in federal employment, a six-month freeze on a scheduled federal pay raise, a 10 percent drop in foreign aid, and deferral of revenue-sharing and welfare-reform.
- A one-year speed-up of increases in personal income tax exemptions and the minimum standard deduction.
- Establishment of a cabinet-level Cost of Living Council to administer the freeze and recommend measures to stabilize wages and prices beyond the 90-day period.
- A floating dollar (the dollar had been locked in place for almost 40 years).

The program went into effect immediately upon its unveiling, so wages and prices would not be raised in anticipation of controls.

The freeze covered virtually all wages and prices, including merit and longevity increases; cost-of-living increases; used goods prices; professional services fees; commission and piece rates; insurance rates; common carrier and utility rates; and motel and hotel prices. Those merchants who paid the extra surcharges were, however, allowed to pass on the surcharges by raising prices accordingly.

Raw agricultural products and finished imports were excluded, the first because of the volatility of supplies and the possibility of shortages, and the latter because the price of imports was judged too difficult to control.

Stock and bond prices and pension increases were also exempted, as were interest rates and dividends (though the President requested that they be held steady).

Prices of new products were to be set according to the most comparable product sold by the closest comparable competitor. Wages of new jobs were to be based on comparable jobs within the business or firm, or comparable jobs in nearby firms.

The freeze caught many companies and unions in especially vulnerable positions. The wages of unions that hadn't yet ratified new contracts — or hadn't yet received their new wages — were automatically frozen. And companies preparing to raise prices were unable to do so. This resulted in a squeeze for some companies. For example, the 450,000 members of the Communications Workers of America had just been granted a 15 percent raise, but Bell Telephone System's request to the Federal Communications Commission for higher tolls to pay for those raises hadn't yet been acted upon, so rates were frozen at the old levels for at least 90 days.

Though the program was described as voluntary, and lacked the huge enforcement bureaucracy characteristic of past wage and price control efforts, the policies were enforceable, and anyone caught raising wages or prices was subject to a $5,000 fine.

It was the first time wage and price controls had been used in the United States since President Truman introduced them in 1951, after prices had climbed 8 percent in an eight-month period.

Domestic reaction to Nixon's proposal was overwhelmingly positive. Leaders of the nation's corporate giants, believing that some sort of action was overdue, responded with general enthusiasm, and opinion polls showed broad support among the populace.

Financial markets reacted with unprecedented gains, as trading on the New York Stock Exchange hit a record 31.72 million shares, and the Dow Jones Industrial Average set a one-day record by climbing 33 points. Bond prices also rose sharply in heavy trading, and prices of commodity futures experienced similar increases.

Labor leaders, however, reacted with undiluted hostility, charging that the policy discriminated against working men and women. In the days that followed the announcement, strikers across the country defied the administration's pleas that they return to work until the freeze ended. A.F.L.-C.I.O. President George Meany announced that his organization would not cooperate with the freeze, and said that workers whose benefits were affected by the freeze should feel free to walk off the job because their contracts had been nullified by the President's action.

Overseas reaction was generally anxious, because of both the 10 percent import surcharge and the floating dollar. Foreign stock markets experienced precipitous drops, and all major world trading centers except Japan halted official international currency dealings.

In the weeks following the introduction of the controls, confusion grew. Development of the Cost of Living Council was not rapid enough to handle all the questions generated by the new regulations, and there was a great deal of uncertainty as to what would follow the 90-day period.

The same business leaders who applauded the intent of the freeze soon began complaining that the confusion it engendered made planning and day-to-day management extremely difficult. Many companies also reported that orders had slowed because customers were uncertain over how they would be affected by the freeze.

As Wilbur Mills, chairman of the House Ways and Means Committee, put it: "The main reservation I have is what follows the 90 days? Something will have to follow the freeze."

Phase II

On October 7, more than a month before the 90-day freeze ended, President Nixon moved to end the state of suspended animation by announcing Phase II.

Phase II widened the scope of the controls by adding profits, dividends and interest, thereby addressing one of labor's chief complaints. The program remained voluntary, but, unlike the freeze, had no cut-off date.

The Cost of Living Council retained its authority over the regulations, but a Pay Board and a Price Commission were established beneath it to set guidelines for wage and price increases, issue orders, and hear cases. The 13-member Pay Board included representatives of business, labor and the general public, while the five members of the Price Commission were all drawn from the public.

There was also an Interest and Dividends Committee, charged with the task of keeping residential mortgage and consumer interest rates at or below current levels, and holding annual dividend increases to 3 percent. In addition, the President created committees on productivity, rent, health services, and state and local government.

Phase II exemptions included raw food products; exports and imports after the first sale; small domestic rental units; and farm, industrial and non-residential property. A few months later, exemptions were also granted to retail firms with sales below $100,000 and firms — excepting those in health and construction — with 60 or less employees.

Both the Pay Board and the Price Commission had variable regulatory requirements depending on company size. The Pay Board administered controls as follows:

- Economic units with more than 5,000 workers had to submit any pay adjustments, in advance, for the Board's approval.
- Those with 1,000 to 5,000 employees could institute pay increases immediately, but had to report them to the Board, which could order that increases be rolled back.
- Those with fewer than 1,000 workers did not have to report wage changes, but were subject to spot inspections to ensure compliance.

The Price Commission requirements were:

- Businesses with annual sales over $100 million had to apply for price increases in advance, and had to file quarterly reports on sales, costs, prices and profits.
- Those with annual sales between $50 and $100 million could raise prices but had to report the increases, which were subject to possible roll-back. These firms also had to file quarterly reports on sales, costs, prices and profits.
- Those with sales below $50 million did not have to report price changes, but were subject to spot checks.

The Price Commission, which was given 3,000 IRS agents to handle enforcement, set a general guideline of 2.5 percent for the average price increase.

Where large companies with varied product lines were concerned, the Price Commission tended to grant across-the-board average increases rather than item-by-item increases. This gave such companies more latitude in adjusting their prices, so long as their aggregate increase remained under the percentage they were granted.

Profits also fell within the realm of Phase II regulation. The regulations allowed a company to raise its prices only if its current pretax profit margins were below its average margin during any two of the company's last three fiscal years. The Price Commission threatened price rollbacks for firms with excessive profit margins.

The Price Commission had 30 days to act on a price increase request, after which it could automatically take effect. Under special circumstances, it was required to act within 72 hours.

The Pay Board, meanwhile, set a 5.5 percent guideline for wage increases, including fringe benefits. The difference between this figure and the 2.5 percent price increase guideline was supposed to equal the long-term trend of increase in productivity.

The wage guidelines included a loophole — the "equity clause" — to correct inequities or substandard conditions. Companies were also allowed to grant increases above 5.5 percent to individuals, so long as their annual aggregate increase didn't exceed that figure.

Wages lost during the 90-day freeze were not to be paid retroactively. Increases scheduled under existing multi-year contracts were allowed if not "unreasonably inconsistent" with the general guidelines.

Companies that signed wage contracts prior to Phase I were generally allowed to pass their additional costs on through price increases. Those that signed contracts after Phase I had been announced were usually limited to recovering only a portion of those higher costs.

Phase III

On January 11, 1973, a little over a year after Phase II was introduced, President Nixon began to remove the controls, disbanding the Price Commission and Pay Board and returning administrative responsibility to the Cost of Living Council.

Most of the changes made in Phase III were in the direction of allowing larger increases. Limits on profit margins were removed, workers earning below $3.50 an hour were exempted, and all rental properties were exempted.

Phase III controls were entirely self-administered. Businesses were asked to interpret the general rules themselves, and reporting requirements were relaxed.

Freeze II and Phase IV

As soon as Phase III began to ease controls, prices began to climb skyward. The food index, for example, rose at a 30 percent annualized rate over the first three months of Phase III.

As a result, the second wage and price freeze was imposed in June 1973, this one to last 60 rather than 90 days.

Two months later, Phase IV was introduced. This was to be the end of the controls, which were now being dropped sector by sector. At the outset, exemptions were expanded to include public utilities, long-term coal contracts, and lumber and copper scrap. Throughout the life of Phase IV, relatively unimportant markets were added to the exemption list. The controllers also attempted to reach agreements with significant industries, offering decontrol in exchange for voluntary price restraint.

With the exception of petroleum prices, the controls were dropped in April 1974, almost three years after the original 90-day freeze was announced.

Impact

Much like the South American experience with controls, the U.S. regulations of the early 1970s created headaches for U.S. companies, and led to circumvention and shortages.

While the controls generally helped industries facing foreign competition, they created problems for businesses that relied on imports, and caused a wide variety of labor difficulties. In addition, the regulations gave rise to a great deal of red tape and confusion, and exerted a significant degree of control, especially over the affairs of larger corporations.

In submitting requests for wage and price increases, the companies that provided the most information generally fared best in having their requests granted. Many submissions were returned with demands for more information, further slowing the approval process.

After the first freeze ended and Phase II began, some companies — especially the large conglomerates — still did not ask for increases at the outset because of the huge job of compiling all the necessary data. Many companies even set up Phase II staffs to administer regulations.

There was also plentiful evidence that companies circumvented the controls. Some of the more widely publicized allegations included:
- Daisy chains, in which goods were bought and resold, often in swap agreements, for the sole reason that each dealer could add a mark-up.

- Labor contracts in which wage increases were held below the ceiling but benefits were increased.
- Cattle were exported to Canada and then reimported to the U.S., because the price of imported beef was uncontrolled.
- Steel makers eliminated the middle of their three grades, forcing middle-grade customers to buy the top line instead.
- Quality deterioration in the lumber industry, most notably changes in plywood dimensions and specifications.
- Overcharging on parts by auto dealers.

While the original 90-day freeze was widely popular, shortages experienced during the second freeze — especially in beef and textiles — resulted in dissatisfaction and a general call for decontrol.

After they were suspended, the controls were generally looked upon as unsuccessful. Though they may have reduced inflation temporarily, any short-term benefit was offset by the climb in rates that followed the suspension of controls. Prices rose at an average annual rate of about 6 percent while the controls were in effect, but in the eight months following the end of Phase IV, they climbed at an annualized rate of over 12 percent.

Suggested Background Reading

"Alfonsin Faces a Hostile Argentine Army," *The Wall Street Journal*, October 29, 1986.

"Anatomy of Failure: The Collapse of Brazil's Cruzado Plan," *The Wall Street Journal*, February 13, 1987, p. 25.

"Argentina, Brazil Woes Continue. Both Economies Still Flounder Following Myriad Reforms," *The Washington Post*, June 20, 1986.

"Argentina Freezes Wages and Prices, Devalues Currency 7 Percent Against Dollar," *The Wall Street Journal*, February 26, 1988.

"Argentina Gets $661 Million IMF Loan; Additional $1.4 Billion Is Expected Soon," *The Wall Street Journal*, July 13, 1987.

"Argentina Looks to Stem the Flow of Emigrants," *The Wall Street Journal*, March 20, 1987, p. 11.

Bace, Lynn A., Edward H. Schwallie, and Gary W. Silverman. *Coping With Inflation: Experiences of Financial Executives in the United Kingdom, Brazil and West Germany.* New York: Financial Executives Research Foundation, 1981.

Baer, Werner. *The Resurgence of Inflation in Brazil: 1974-1985.* University of Illinois at Urbana - Champaign.

Banco De Boston. *Newsletter Argentina.* Years 1986, 1987, 1988.

Banco De Boston. *Newsletter Brazil.* Years 1986, 1987, 1988.

Banerjee, Mrityunjoy. *Inflation: Causes and Cures.* Calcutta: The World Press Private Limited, 1975.

Banyai, Richard A. *The Legal and Monetary Aspects of the Hungarian Hyper-Inflation 1945-1946.* Phoenix: 1971.

"Barometer Falling," *Forbes*, September 7, 1987, pp. 32-33.

"Bolivia Tries to Rebound," *The Christian Science Monitor,* August 6, 1987.

"Brazil Debt Woes Echo Those of Region," *The Wall Street Journal,* December 1, 1986, p. 20.

"Brazil Hardens Its Position on Paying Debt," *The Wall Street Journal,* February 26, 1988, p. 25.

"Brazil Learns a Little Humility," *The Economist,* June 20, 1987, pp. 79-80.

"Brazil Report," *Latin American Regional Reports,* London: Latin American Newsletter Ltd, September 18, 1986, pp. 1-8.

"Brazil Ties Payback to Talks With Banks," *The Arizona Daily Star,* February 22, 1987, pp. 1, 6A.

"Brazil to End Cruzado Plan's Freeze on Prices," *The Wall Street Journal,* December 18, 1986.

"Brazil. Tomorrow's Italy," *The Economist,* January 17, 1987, pp. 19-22.

"Brazil's Crippling Inflation," *The New York Times,* May 30, 1987.

"Brazil's Dream Remains on Hold," *Insight,* August 17, 1987, pp. 8-19.

"Brazil's Land Reform Condemns Farmers to Poverty," *The Wall Street Journal,* May 20, 1988, p. 25.

"Brazil's President Isn't Likely to Impose Austerity Needed to Get Through Crisis," *The Wall Street Journal,* February 25, 1987, p. 30.

Bresciani-Turroni, Costantino. *The Economics of Inflation. A Study of Currency Depreciation in Post-War Germany.* London: George Allen and Unwin Ltd., 1937.

Brown, A.J., and Jane Darby. *World Inflation Since 1950. An International Comparative Study.* Cambridge: Cambridge University Press, 1985.

"A Burdened Land Searching for the Heart of Progress," *Insight,* August 17, 1987, pp. 15-17.

Cagan, Phillip. *Persistent Inflation. Historical and Policy Essays.* New York: Columbia University Press, 1979.

Cardoso, Eliana A. "Latin America's Debt: Which Way Now?," *Challenge,* May/June 1987, pp. 11-17.

Cohen, Robert. "Brazil's Economic Crisis Could Lead to Delay of Payments on Foreign Debt," *The Wall Street Journal,* February 17, 1987.

The Columbia Journal of World Business, XXI, No. 3 (Fall 1986).

"A Crusader Unveils Rampant Pay Perks in a Brazilian State," *The Wall Street Journal,* February 25, 1988, pp. 1, 20.

"Disenchantment Grows Over Argentina's Inflation Fight," *The Los Angeles Times,* June 16, 1986.

Eder, George Jackson. *Inflation and Development in Latin America. A Case History of Inflation and Stabilization in Bolivia.* Michigan: The Bureau of Business Research, Graduate School of Business Administration, The University of Michigan, 1968.

Edgerton, Jerry, Junius Ellis, and Jordan E. Goodman. "Why Investors Fear Renewed Inflation," *Money,* June 1988, pp. 11-12.

The First Boston Corporation. "The Brazil Fund, Inc. Common Stock," *Prospectus,* March 11, 1988, pp. 1-65.

Friedman, Irving S. *Inflation a World-Wide Disaster.* Boston: Houghton Mifflin Company, 1973.

"Full Stop: End to 'Dirty War' Era," *Insight,* January 26, 1987, pp. 38-39.

Gresham, Otto. *The Greenbacks or the Money That Won the Civil War and the World War.* Chicago: The Book Press Inc., 1927.

Hahn, Frank. *Money and Inflation.* Cambridge: The MIT Press, 1981.

Harteneck, Lopez y Cia. *Summary of Business Conditions in Argentina.* Buenos Aires: Coopers and Lybrand, November 1985.

"How One Economist Tries to Keep Abreast of Third World Trends," *The Wall Street Journal,* January 2, 1987, pp. 1, 8.

Humphrey, Thomas M. *Essays on Inflation.* 5th ed. Richmond: Federal Reserve Bank of Richmond, 1986.

"Is Depression the Only Cure for Inflation?," *Forbes,* March 1, 1975, pp. 20-22, 27.

Jud, Gustav Donald. *Inflation and the Use of Indexing in Developing Countries.* New York: Praeger Publishers, 1978.

Kahil, Raouf. *Inflation and Economic Development in Brazil.* Oxford: Clarendon Press, 1973.

"Latin American Debtors Are Spoiling for a Fight," *International Business,* May 27, 1985, pp. 52-53.

"Latin Crisis, As Debt Turmoil Ebbs and Flows in Mexico, Human Misery Persists," *The Wall Street Journal,* June 12, 1986, pp. 1, 23.

Leijonhufvud, Axel. *Information and Coordination Essays in Macroeconomic Theory.* New York: Oxford University Press, 1981.

Maese, Judy E. and Clark A. Hawkins. "A Current Perspective on the Latin American Debt Situation: Can the Debt Problem Be Managed?," *New Mexico Business Forum*, Spring 1988.

Martone, Celso L. *Macroeconomic Policies, Debt Accumulation, and Adjustment in Brazil, 1965-84.* Washington, D.C.: The World Bank, 1987.

McKeogh, Richard, and Juan Carlos Herken-Krauer. "Argentina to 1992. The Search for Solutions," *EIU Economic Prospects Series.* London: The Economist Intelligence Unit. Special Report No. 1102, pp. 1-101.

"Mexican President Faces No-Win Situation," *The Wall Street Journal,* June 13, 1986, p. 19.

Parsson, Jens O. *Dying of Money.* Boston: Wellspring Press, 1974.

"Precarious Pesos, Amid Wild Inflation, Bolivians Concentrate on Swapping Currency," *The Wall Street Journal,* August 13, 1985.

Remarque, Erich Maria. *The Black Obelisk.* New York: Harcourt Brace and World, Inc., 1957.

"Rich and Poor a Door Apart," *Insight,* August 17, 1987, pp. 18-19.

Riding, Alan. "Brazil's Crippling Inflation," *The New York Times,* May 30, 1987.

Riding, Alan. "Disillusioned Brazil Awakes From a Dream of Prosperity," *The New York Times,* December 6, 1987, pp. 1, 28.

Ringer, Fritz K., ed. *The German Inflation of 1923.* New York: Oxford University Press, 1969.

Roberts, Paul Craig. "The Debt Crisis Isn't Brazil's Only Liability," *Business Week,* April 20, 1987, p. 14.

Rosen, Harvey S., and Wilma St. John, eds. *The American Economic Review.* Vol. 77, No. 2. Menasha: American Economic Association, 1987.

Samuelson, Larry. *Inflation, Indexing, and Economic Development.* Department of Economics, Pennsylvania State University.

Sargent, Thomas J. *Rational Expectations and Inflation.* New York: Harper and Row, 1986.

Savidis, George, ed. *C.P. Cavafy Collected Poems.* Princeton: Princeton University Press, 1975.

Schmukler, Nathan, and Edward Marcus, eds. *Inflation Through the Ages: Economic, Social, Psychological and Historical Aspects.* New York: Columbia University Press, 1983.

Schuettinger, Robert L., and Eamonn F. Butler. *Forty Centuries of Wage and Price Controls: How Not to Fight Inflation.* New York: Caroline House Publishers, Inc., 1979.

Shapiro, Max. *The Penniless Billionaires.* New York: Truman Talley Books, 1980.

Solomon, Anthony M. "A Declining Dollar is Just One Piece in the Puzzle," *Business Week,* April 13, 1987, p. 20.

Solow, Robert M. "What We Know and Don't Know About Inflation," *Technology Review,* December/January 1979, pp. 31-46.

Sommers, Albert T. *Inflation: The Crucial Challenge in the 1980's.* New York: The Conference Board, Inc., Report No. 798.

"Southern Cone Report." *Latin American Regional Reports.* London: Latin American Newsletters Ltd, March 10, 1988, pp. 1-8.

"Southern Cone Report." *Latin American Regional Reports.* London: Latin American Newsletters Ltd, April 21, 1988, pp. 1-8.

Stone, Gerald, and Ralph Byrns. *The Hyperinflation Collection.* 16675, Third Edition. Scott, Foresman and Company, pp. 1-5.

"A Swelling Tide of Troubles," *Time,* February 23, 1987, p. 60.

Truell, Peter, and Roger Cohen. "Brazil Debt Action Poses Challenge for Major Banks," *The Wall Street Journal,* February 23, 1987, pp. 3, 20.

Verzarju, Pompiliu. *International Countertrade: A Guide for Managers and Executives.* Washington, D.C.: U.S. Department of Commerce, International Trade Administration, November 1984.

Vesilind, Pritt J. "Moment of Promise and Pain," *National Geographic,* March 1987, pp. 352-384.

"Volcker Warns of Debt-Crisis 'Fatigue,' Says Brazilian Growth Can Cover Loans," *The Wall Street Journal,* February 25, 1987, p. 2A.

Whitney, Simon N. *Inflation Since 1945. Facts and Theories.* New York: Praeger Publishers, 1982.

Williamson, John, ed. *Inflation and Indexation. Argentina, Brazil, and Israel.* Cambridge: MIT Press, 1985.

World Bank, The. *1986-87 World Debt Tables. Second Supplement. External Debt of Developing Countries.* Washington, D.C.: The World Bank, 1987.

"Your Money or Your Life," *The Economist,* February 28, 1987, pp. 37-38.